To Christian and Rachel

I am, because you are.

Contents

Bounce

how to raise resilient kids and teens

NAOMI HOLDT

GREEN TREE

GREEN TREE
Bloomsbury Publishing Plc
50 Bedford Square, London, WC1B 3DP, UK
Bloomsbury Publishing Ireland Limited,
29 Earlsfort Terrace, Dublin 2, D02 AY28, Ireland

BLOOMSBURY, GREEN TREE and the Green Tree logo are trademarks of
Bloomsbury Publishing Plc

First published in 2023 in South Africa as Bounce
by Pan Macmillan South Africa
First published in Great Britain 2026

Bloomsbury Publishing Plc does not have any control over, or responsibility for,
any third-party websites referred to or in this book. All internet addresses given
in this book were correct at the time of going to press. The author and publisher
regret any inconvenience caused if addresses have changed or sites have ceased
to exist, but can accept no responsibility for any such changes

A catalogue record for this book is available from the British Library

Library of Congress Cataloguing-in-Publication data has been applied for

ISBN: TPB: 978-1-3994-2739-5; eBook: 978-1-3994-2740-1

2 4 6 8 10 9 7 5 3 1

Typeset by Nyx Design
Printed and bound in Great Britain by Clays Ltd, Elcograf S.p.A.

To find out more about our authors and books visit www.bloomsbury.com and
sign up for our newsletters
For product safety related questions contact productsafety@bloomsbury.com

PART 3: BY THE WAY

A Bit about Me

Before you begin reading this book, you should probably know a little bit about who I am and what I do.

Beyond titles and qualifications, I am a mom to two deeply empathic children. I am a parent, just like you, one who messes things up and gets it wrong at times; one who has learnt to smile at her faults, learn from her mistakes, and see through it all to discover the immense joy that this unpredictable, roller-coaster ride of raising children brings along with it. At the time of writing this book, my son was ten years old and my daughter was eight. I have been working with children in various contexts for almost three decades – through my days as a youth leader, an educator, a psychologist and a mother. Still, I am privileged to learn from children and teens every single day. They have been, and remain, my greatest teachers in life.

This book is the real-deal, true-life stories from my own home and my psychotherapy practice. I have *loved* putting it together for you and my hope is that what you read on these pages enriches your own journey and significantly deepens your relationship with your child.

This quote by Elizabeth Gilbert sums up a great deal about our parenting adventure:

'Having a child is like getting a tattoo on your face. You better be committed.'

By picking up this book, you've already proven how ready you are for the commitment you've been given.

Thanks for choosing to venture through this journey with me.

With love,
Naomi

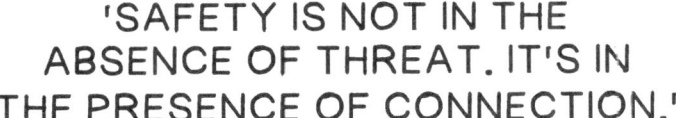

'SAFETY IS NOT IN THE
ABSENCE OF THREAT. IT'S IN
THE PRESENCE OF CONNECTION.'
Gabor Maté

Preface

If you are looking for an 'academic'-type book that's filled with statistics, equations and hard data, this book is *not* for you. Please put it down and try the next one on the shelf in the parenting section.

This book is written for parents and caregivers by a very *real* parent, who also happens to be a psychologist and who, over the past few decades, has worked with thousands of children, teens and parents. This book is based on my journey with my own children and experience in my psychology practice and in it I give many 'real-life' examples that I am hoping will resonate with you exactly where you are in your parenting journey too. Our families and circumstances of our parenting journeys may all look very different, but there are so many similarities along this most challenging yet most important role of life that we have been given.

I am privileged to work psychotherapeutically with phenomenal children, teens and parents and walk the road alongside them towards healing whatever life issues they may be struggling with.

These pages are loaded with tons of practical ideas and 'mirror questions' (the hard parenting ones we need to ask ourselves and answer honestly in order for us to be who our children need us to be).

This book is meant to be an easy-reading, meaningful parenting guide, delivered in digestible bite-sized nuggets that will leave you feeling empowered and ready to tackle this messy and beautiful journey of life and parenting.

Allow this book to also serve as a 'workbook' of sorts that will give you space to do a bit of self-reflection. Not just the feel-good kind. The *hard* kind that leads to powerful shifts and positive changes in the relationship you have with your child.

I hope that the words printed on these pages will help you move from 'What the heck do I do now?' to 'I've got this!' even if your voice trembles slightly as you declare it.

Here's a compassionate reminder:

 REMINDER: No one — absolutely no one — has this life, let alone the parenting thing, all figured out.

No matter how many textbooks and manuals we have at our disposal, we all mess up. From time to time, we'll all find our faces planted in the sand. The truth is that most of us are frantically paddling while trying to maintain the picture of calm and make sense of this journey as we attempt to raise happy, healthy and resilient kids.

Parenting is filled with beautiful moments – moments of connection, moments of magic and moments that create memories that shape the foundations of our children's souls. Equally, parenting is hard – it's tough, it's exhausting and at times, it's even heartbreaking ...

On that note, I'd like to remind you of three words. Write them in big and bold text on your mirror, set a daily reminder alarm using them as the title, have them as your screensaver:

I'M NOT ALONE.

In between the magical moments and soulful connections with our children, we all have 'good parent' days, 'bad parent' days, days we long to throw the duvet back over our heads and pretend the world doesn't exist for 24 hours, and days that we wish we could have a complete do-over.

Our paths may *look* different but none of us is perfect, including the 'parenting professionals' (like me) with decades of experience under our belts. If you're a parent looking for affirmation that you're not the only one who messes up occasionally, and you want some practical and ground-level ideas from a real-life mom-psychologist, then keep reading.

PS Whenever I use the word 'parent', please know that I also really mean any caregivers and guardians working with or caring for children and teens in any way.

>Introduction<

My Reality Check

Undeniably, our world has remained on its head for the last few years. Unpredictable, chaotic and frantic. Let's just say that the number of 'unknowns' and variables has hit astronomical levels. It's hard enough for us as adults trying to navigate all of this uncertainty, but for our kids and teens whose brains are still in 'development mode', it's been merciless.

Looking back in history, there has never been a time when rotten lemons weren't tossed in the direction of the human race. It's this journey called life. We're in it and we know it tends to deliver quite the sucker punch at the most unexpected times. We'll get knocked down despite every defence weapon we have in our arsenal and we'd do well to remember that our kids will go down at some stage too.

The good news is that it doesn't end there and our kids don't have to stay face down in that pile of dirt they'll inevitably find themselves in.

You're probably jumping at the question popping up in your head, 'But, Naomi, how do we as parents ensure that despite these lemon-drenched sucker punches our kids will get back up again?'

For me the 'big' questions surrounding all things relating to our kids and their resilience began during 2010. I conducted an educational assessment on a 14-year-old boy (let's call him Mark) who had significant academic difficulties. Apart from his learning challenges, I also noted severe depression and in my feedback session with his parents, I recommended he be treated with medication and psychotherapy. To my knowledge, his parents followed through on these suggestions. I heard nothing more from Mark and his family after the feedback session until about eight months later. I received an email from one of Mark's extended family members. It was short, concise and delivered the most tragic news.

Mark had taken his own life.

I was devastated. A young man who passed through the doors of my practice had taken one knock too many, one knock too hard, one knock from which he could not get back up.

Mark was not born depressed. No child is.

In fact, as a young child he was happy and energetic. The questions began to roll in like an avalanche. What was it that led a young man who was once a child just like yours, just like mine, to become so disillusioned with life that he no longer felt it was worth staying alive or getting back up?

What can we do in our homes to solidify resilience in our

children and teens to give them the best chance of developing into happy and emotionally healthy young humans?

The increasing thought momentum around this enormous topic led me to the same simple conclusions and I feel privileged to be able to share them with you in this book.

Many parents I work with want 'the toolkit', the DIY, the plug-and-play-type checklist that contains 'characteristics to build'. This is not that kind of book. This is *not* a book that fills your brain with new scientific information and it won't give you that toolkit that you so desperately *think* you need.

Instead, I hope the words on these pages leave you with something even better – simple reminders of everyday things that you can change in your home with minimal effort that will make a powerful difference in your child's life and in your relationship with them. It's going to leave you feeling confident that YOU CAN DO THIS! You CAN raise a resilient child who, because of the relationship you build with them, will be able to dodge those lemons and if, by chance, they slip on the odd peel, they'll have what it takes to get back up.

The secret sauce in this resilience recipe – as you read on – is YOU. That is the exciting part. I'm not going to suggest you change anything that's beyond your potential. The changes you make can be implemented straight away and those changes begin with you. In a world where so much is uncertain, it is empowering as a parent to know 'It all starts with me'. The little things that you say and do have the power to completely change the trajectory of your child's life. This reminder right here may feel like an extremely overwhelming responsibility. Keep reading. You've 'got this' way more than you think you do.

One very important nugget of information that I need to emphasise is: I, just like you, am a human parent. A very human one. You'll realise as you read this book that I 'mess up' plenty of times. I frequently revisit the aspects I speak about in this book and invariably need to remind myself of them and when I do, it makes *all* the difference to my connection with my kids. That, as you'll learn, is the strongest foundation of resilience for us all: CONNECTION within a healthy attached relationship.

'LIFE IS NOT ABOUT HOW FAST YOU RUN, OR HOW HIGH YOU CLIMB BUT HOW WELL YOU BOUNCE.'

Vivian Komori

I'm excited that you've chosen to join me on this journey to help you learn how to ensure that, as far as possible, our homes are elasticised places in which our children and teens can learn to bounce.

PART 1
The Background

Where It All Begins ...

Life changes forever the day you hold your newborn baby in your arms. From the second you touch that soft skin and the moment you look into your little one's eyes for the first time, life will never be the same again. You can read a library of books before this pivotal moment, attend as many seminars as possible, calmly breathe your way through birthing classes, show up at a plethora of baby workshops, watch your best friends' children grow up, and babysit your nieces and nephews. You can do all of that, but nothing can prepare you for the day that you become responsible for bringing life into the world. From that moment, a different kind of determination is awakened in you, a ferocity that can sometimes frighten you, a tiger and tigress you may never have realised existed within you.

Just one second and it all changes – it's no longer about you ... ever again.

Everything from this point on becomes all about that little person and you'll single-mindedly do everything in your power to ensure their physical and emotional survival. No matter how old they are, this fierce determination continues. It's ingrained in you.

Parenting is one of the hardest, often most crippling journeys that we will ever walk. Truthfully, it's also one of the most disempowering.

It's one where we're sometimes forced to watch helplessly as our kids face the inevitable challenges that come their way. As parents we are hardwired to protect our children, but the most difficult part is that sometimes we can't cushion their fall, we can't stop them from getting hurt, and we can't stop them from experiencing pain. There are plenty of things in this world that are going to knock our children to the ground. These could include friendship issues, not getting picked for the sports team, doing badly in a test, being a victim of crime, experiencing trauma, the death of a loved one, parents' divorce, parental discord, bullying, drugs, alcohol, anxiety and depression. This list is naturally not exhaustive and I'm sure you have your own personal examples that you could add.

However varied these may be, they share a common denominator – they are extreme pain points for us as parents and the most challenging part is that oftentimes all we can do is watch helplessly from the sidelines flexing our – as I like to call them – 'tiger muscles'. (These are the muscles we develop as parents that unleash a fiercely protective side in all of us and can give us sleepless nights.)

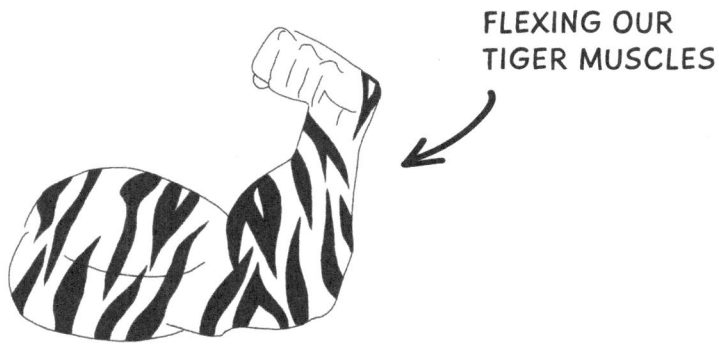

FLEXING OUR
TIGER MUSCLES

PARENTING THROUGH THE GENERATIONS

Never before has there been a generation of children that has been more over-parented and under-protected. Helicopter parenting, tiger parenting, snow-plough parenting, free-range parenting and more. Every part of our children's lives is 'overbooked', oversubscribed and micromanaged and we live in fear that we're still making a complete mess of raising them.

Parenting has certainly gone through multiple metamorphoses over the past few decades. Our grandparents may have handed our parents over to nannies. Parenting was more often an 'occasional' interaction and the only expectation of children was to be 'seen and not heard'. Think stay-out-of-the-drawing-room-while-the-adults-drink-whiskey-type situation.

Our parents shifted gears a little. When they brought us home they kept 'adulting' with other adults and pretty much leaving us to our own devices. We rode around the neighbourhood on bicycles with friends, stayed outdoors until after dark, religiously went to church on Sundays, drove in cars without seatbelts, played on very risky playground equipment and made our parents ashtrays in art class. Hands-off parenting was the order of the decade.

Then the shift happened again. A transformation and metamorphosis so ruthless and 'hands-on' that it has resulted in over-scheduled diaries, anxious, exhausted and stressed children and parents who feel all of that plus an immense load of guilt.

Even though we are more physically 'present' than ever in our children's lives, we have also never been more disconnected. Combine this with a few global traumas like a pandemic, financial insecurity, national disasters and political instability and we have been left with a generation of anxious and depressed children and teens who lack confidence, a sense of self, and many of the attributes needed for resilience.

The parenting style of the 1960s, 1970s and 1980s was certainly not 'faultless'. That kind of authoritarian parenting of 'I am "God" and you shall do what I say or face hell' (both literally and figuratively) resulted in a cascade of carnage and many broken adults (although few adults will willingly admit this).

We would have hoped by now that with all we have learnt about a child's neurological development and emotional needs somehow we would have got the balance right. We haven't.

We lack resilience ourselves and our children are lacking this essential survival attribute too. We have bubble-wrapped our little precious beings so tightly that we have prevented them from being able to manage any kind of struggle.

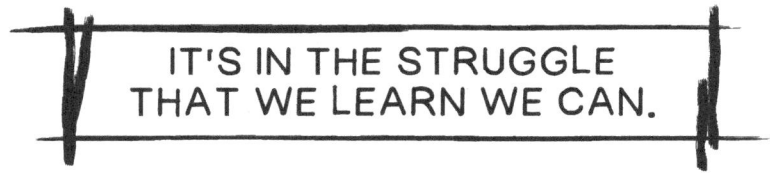

IT'S IN THE STRUGGLE
THAT WE LEARN WE CAN.

Our role in parenting isn't to prevent our children from falling. It's to let them fall, knowing that we are there to support them while they find their way to get back up again.

By attempting to bypass the 'hardship valley' for our kids, we are in fact robbing them of their ability to build resilience. Yes, ROBBING them. That's a tough one, I know. My first instinct as a parent is to jump right in and stretch out that safety net. But I need to constantly remind myself that in doing that, I am contributing significantly to the likelihood that my child will not get up because they will never have learnt that they are capable of recovering without me.

So the question is:

How do we combine lessons learnt from past generations with the knowledge we know to be true from groundbreaking science and research to raise kids in the most effective way to build resilience?

GETTING RIGHT TO IT

Building resilience is not a done-in-a-day, tick-the-box event. It is a continuous journey. Each day our children present us with incredible opportunities to develop and harness these skills that live within them.

The information presented on these pages is relevant to children of *all* ages. If you think that because your child is still young you'll worry about all of this later, know that how you parent your child at a younger age largely determines the type of teens and adults they become. If your kids are already teens, take heart; it's never too late to change our relationship with our children – even our adult ones – and in doing that, we help them develop resilience.

Every day we choose the kind of children we want to be raising. *We* do. Not the world out there, not social media, not the opinion of well-meaning mothers-in-law, not the chatter from car-park moms or beer-club dads. *We* do. Raising children and teens who can navigate the world with courage and bravery begins in the everyday, often seemingly insignificant, choices of what we say and do.

Life is hard, but luckily we can do hard things and ultimately we want our children to believe this with every fibre of their being.

This quote sums up our role as parents:

The Issue of Being Bulletproof

As with the tiger-muscle-flexing analogy, it's ingrained in our parental bones that we are hardwired to protect our children. One of the most devastating and heartbreaking aspects of parenting is realising that, despite our best intentions and all the effort we may go to, our children cannot make the journey through life unscathed and we cannot protect them from what lies ahead. Their 'big wide world' – at school, with friends, at home ...

It's not a matter of whether or not our children will encounter life's hard knocks, it's a matter of whether they're going to survive these knocks both physically and emotionally, and whether they'll come out on the other end relatively unscathed, and even more resilient.

Let's begin by defining the concept of 'emotionally bulletproof' and the meaning behind it. To help us along the way, I want to delve into the world of Netflix for a moment. I used to love the show *Criminal Minds* (until it became way too psychologically freaky for me), but the visual remains powerful.

In these kind of shows the law enforcement guys' standard and essential daily attire includes a bulletproof vest. Picture the scene:

> Good guys (cops) pitch up to a hostile situation. One of our heroes makes a dash across the parking lot. Bullets erupt from the 'bad guy's' weapon and hit one of the good guys.

What's important to remember here is that our good guy doesn't prance through the hail of bullets without a millimetre's deflection to either side. In fact, even when someone is wearing a bulletproof vest and gets shot, the shot knocks them down, and it might even take their breath away.

Back to our scene:

> Good cop goes down and everyone runs over. There's a heart-stopping, wide-eyed moment when onlookers aren't quite sure if our hero's going to make it. But finally the good cop takes that shock 'gasp for breath' and our hero's eyes open.

And with that comes relief! Out comes the breath you've been holding as you release the tight grip on the couch. Phew! It's all going to be okay.

In the same way, by equipping our children with emotional 'bulletproof vests', we are not preventing them from never getting hit. We know that's impossible; it's a part of life for all of us. Even though we wish we could save our little (and big) people from all the pain of the inevitable traumas of life and wrap them in cotton wool forever, sadness, pain and disappointment *will* come their way.

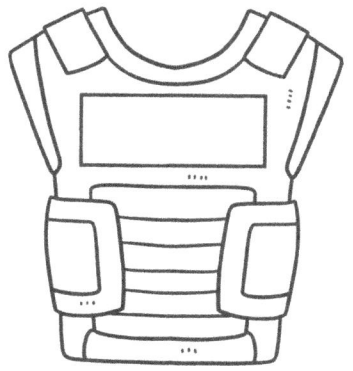

Children who
have been
given the
'bulletproofing'
of resilience get
back up again.

 This is the hard and painful parenting reality, but the difference is that *children who have been given the 'bulletproofing' of resilience get up again.* They come up for that huge gasp of air after getting knocked down and they keep on running.

The Power of Epigenetics

There are so many factors that play a role in shaping our children's resilience. Perhaps some of you may be thinking that because there is a strong genetic predisposition towards depression and anxiety in your family, your child is doomed. This is most certainly not the case. We place so much importance and emphasis on genetics and the role they play in our children's make-up, but when we do that we subconsciously relinquish our control and attribute all responsibility to genes.

Years ago, I treated a 17-year-old boy who I'll call Liam. His treatment plan included helping him deal with some of life's pressures. One day, while chatting about his diagnosis of depression and anxiety, Liam sat back and resignedly told me, 'Everyone in my family suffers from depression and anxiety. My mom, dad, sister. It's just something I take a pill or two for every day and probably always will.'

He was trapped and felt disempowered by his diagnosis. We talked a bit more and I told him, 'Liam, you've become a victim of mental-health diagnoses. They've taken control of you and you've allowed it to happen by believing that there's nothing you can do about it. TAKE BACK YOUR CONTROL!'

This young man had felt completely disempowered and helpless and believed that for the rest of his life he would be controlled and trapped by his diagnosis. That is a scary and disheartening place for anyone to dwell in, let alone a 17-year-old boy. We kept working weekly in therapy for another six months, during which time he was able to gain the skills he needed to manage his mental health. Liam was able to find freedom from that disempowered state as soon as he began to take ownership of it.

Genes do not control every aspect of who we are. In fact, medical research is proving over and over that you can be predisposed to almost any genetic disease, but unless you create the environment for those genes to express themselves and thrive, they are likely to remain suppressed and 'harmless'. It's the environment and NOT the genes that lay the foundation for resilience and as parents we play a tremendous role in creating the home environment that our children grow up in.

If you're a genetics and medically minded type of person, and you're wanting more of that kind of information, the next section is a bite-sized snack just for you.

GENES FOR RESILIENCE

When it comes to resilience, there's a percentage of children who have been given a 'head start', where resilience traits may be partially inherited. Children who are more adaptable by nature, more outgoing and less emotionally reactive often have this advantage. There are two specific genes that scientists have identified that seem to confer some degree of resilience in our children.

These genes are 5-HTTLPR, which influences serotonin, and OPRM1, which promotes attachment. There are many others that have more recently been associated with resilience and, in particular, related to resilience against stress-related psychiatric disorders.

Some of these include:

- Dopamine receptor D4 (DRD4)
- Brain-derived neurotrophic factor (BDNF)
- Corticotropin-releasing hormone receptor 1 (CRHR1)
- Regulator of G-protein signalling 2 (RGS2).

Aside from naming them, I'm not going to try to explain their respective roles any further. I'll leave it up to you to research the widely available studies.

In terms of the very human application of all this scientific information, here's what you need to keep in mind: The critical determining factor is NOT the genes, it's the interaction between genes and their environment. Sensitive parenting can modify the way a child's inherited characteristics are expressed. Some studies even suggest that shy children who receive tuned-in and gentle parenting* are able to use their heightened sensitivity to become phenomenal leaders, yet shy children who are poorly parented may find that they struggle with shyness and even anxiety their whole lives.

 *Gentle parenting: An evidence-based parenting style that incorporates respect and kindness, empathy and boundaries all wrapped up in unconditional love.

MY PERSONAL TWO CENTS' WORTH

My two children are both sensitive empaths. As a young child my son would pick me flowers (he still does) and put them next to my bed. He still draws me pictures and picks up special rocks and natural treasures for me. He is a child who is extremely perceptive of my emotions and has the kindest and most gentle nature. He has a magical soul, but my mother-heart knows that life's going to be just a little bit tougher for him than for his younger sister.

She is the one who bounces in with high-highs and low-lows! She embraces life with a 'head-on' attitude and a strong, fiery will. She's the joker and the entertainer. When she falls, she gets straight back up, both emotionally and physically. She feels the world very deeply but she's feisty and independent.

As a preschooler my son would often ask for help, but when I went down on my knees to help my then two-year-old daughter with something almost impossible for a child of her age to accomplish alone, she would push her finger on to my nose and say, 'No, no, no. I do it.'

They are two completely different children with completely different natures, but it's *my* job to make sure that both are equally capable of getting up after taking a knock. It is *your* job to ensure that no matter your child's character, they are as resilient as possible to whatever life may toss in their direction.

Regardless of a child's genetic make-up you have the power to assist in creating a foundation of resilience for them. Genetics shouldn't be disempowering. The fact that you have control over so many aspects of your child's environment should be EMPOWERING! And that feeling of empowerment is what I want you to walk away with after reading this book.

What Does Resilience Look Like?

I am a visual person, and if you know and love Winnie the Pooh as much as I do, the following analogy will hopefully resonate with you.

Tigger is extremely likeable and he's full of positivity and sunshine. He has the incredible ability to look on the bright side and he bounces around no matter how bumpy his day has been. He's the epitome of resilience. *Boing! Boing! Boing!* ... he bounds through it. If you can't picture or aren't familiar with Tigger, think of an elastic band. You can stretch it pretty far, but time and time again it snaps back to its pre-stretched self. *That* is resilience.

If the formal definition is more your thing, then here it is:

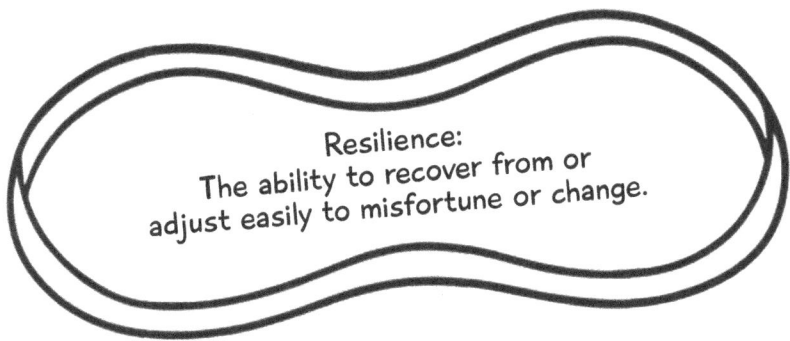

Resilience:
The ability to recover from or adjust easily to misfortune or change.

What we are aiming for here is not an unrealistic picture of *not* being affected by life's challenges, but rather a return to a regulated state when things that we cannot control arise.

The Crazy Knocks

In my early 20s, I decided that I wanted to take up kickboxing. I was a yellow belt when I took part in my first tournament. In martial arts, rating works in belt colours and yellow sits somewhere near the bottom (amateur alert). During tournaments what's most important is that you fight against your weight category, but that day there weren't any other yellow-belt females in my weight category, only a double-dan black belt (super-expert level).

I went into the ring feeling so nervous that I could hear my heart beating in my throat and let's just say I didn't walk out celebrating. I was knocked down (miraculously, not knocked out). Actually, I was slam-dunked, side-kicked, round-house-kicked, jabbed ... You name the move, she hardly missed a shot and my attempts at blocking were, well, not very successful. That's what happens in life sometimes. It's not only going to knock us and our children down completely, it's going to result in us crashing to the ground. Hard. I got back up that day and resolved that I never wanted to be in that position again. I trained hard most days and managed to achieve my black belt 18 months later. Although I didn't realise it at the time, now that I study and work with young people's brain development on a daily basis, I can recognise that my mother's influence laid the foundation for me to have resilience developed within me. For that I will be forever grateful.

But why is it that some children who've experienced trauma and hardship in their lives are so resilient and seem to bounce back from everything while there are others who seem to be scarred for life? What makes that difference?

Well, remember those rotten lemons? We're going to learn to make lemonade with them. Pay attention because this book is not about things your *children* need to change. It is to help bring about a realisation in you of the attributes and characteristics *you* need to help them develop into happier adults. It's about how we can make a difference in the way we parent our children. It's about how we can change things for our children. Truth bomb: It's not about our children. It's about *us*.

We're going to learn how to make lemonade!

Stand in front of the mirror. Look at yourself. If you want to raise a resilient child, the work must start with and happen ... IN YOU.

Parenting has much more to do with the work within ourselves than it does with our children.

Although that sentence seems like quite a daunting realisation, remember that simple, powerful changes you can make within your home can bring about significant positive outcomes for your child. Try not to feel overwhelmed at any stage. Don't tell yourself you're never going to be able to implement all these suggestions, but still want a resilient child. Don't get yourself into a tizz and become derailed and feel like your situation is hopeless. I frequently feel overwhelmed by many things in my life. Pause. Breathe. Remember that change *is* possible.

THE SIGNIFICANCE OF ONE DEGREE

If an aeroplane takes off but adjusts its flight path by just one degree, it will end up at a *completely* different destination as to where it was originally meant to be. A completely different place. A flight from Los Angeles heading directly to Rome is an arduous,

12-hour flight. If the nose of the aeroplane is pointed just one degree off to the south, the plane will arrive somewhere in Tunisia. One tiny difference over a long period of `time + distance = an entirely different outcome` (and on a totally different continent).

Rather than trying to remember everything you need to change and becoming so overwhelmed that you abandon it all, choose one small change at a time. One degree is going to mean an entirely different landing spot when it comes to your relationship with your child and their resilience. When broken down like this, it should bring you some relief. One degree. That's your focus.

A LITTLE REFRAMING WHEN IT COMES TO 'BEHAVIOUR'

There's so much that we need to remember when it comes to understanding our children's behaviour and the connection to their mental health. External behaviour is always a reflection of what's happening in our child's internal world, which is why it always goes beyond 'This behaviour needs chastising!' Actually, no. This behaviour needs understanding. Either it's completely developmentally appropriate behaviour given your child's developmental stage or – and this is important – our kids and teens are sending out smoke signals and crying out for help. They need connection. They need to feel safe.

Every type of behaviour sends us one of two messages: 'I am feeling safe and all is well in my world' or 'Things are chaotic and rattled up in here. Please help me'.

The behaviour that you think is 'unruly' and needs 'discipline' confirms how much of an upside-down world our kids and teens feel like they are living in. The naked truth is that they *don't* feel safe. They're coming to YOU to ask for help.

Keep reading. Things will become clearer.

Ground Level

In recent years there's been a significant increase in anxiety and depression across the globe and our kids and teens have not been spared. At grassroots level, and in homes and classrooms, parents and educators are reporting behaviours such as increased meltdowns, greater separation anxiety, heightened anger, a lack of motivation and rebellious defiance.

We're seeing a rise in boundary testing, 'impossible behaviours', greater distractibility and impulsivity, lower tolerance levels, increased sensitivity, more attention-seeking behaviours (and what may for some parents feel like highly annoying ones such as whining, clinging and 'floor dropping'). Finally, and not surprisingly, there's the ugly side to all of this: the higher rates of substance abuse, eating disorders, self-harm and suicidal ideation.

I (sadly) have a front-row, 4D seat to this in my psychology practice.

But what does resilience have to do with all of this?

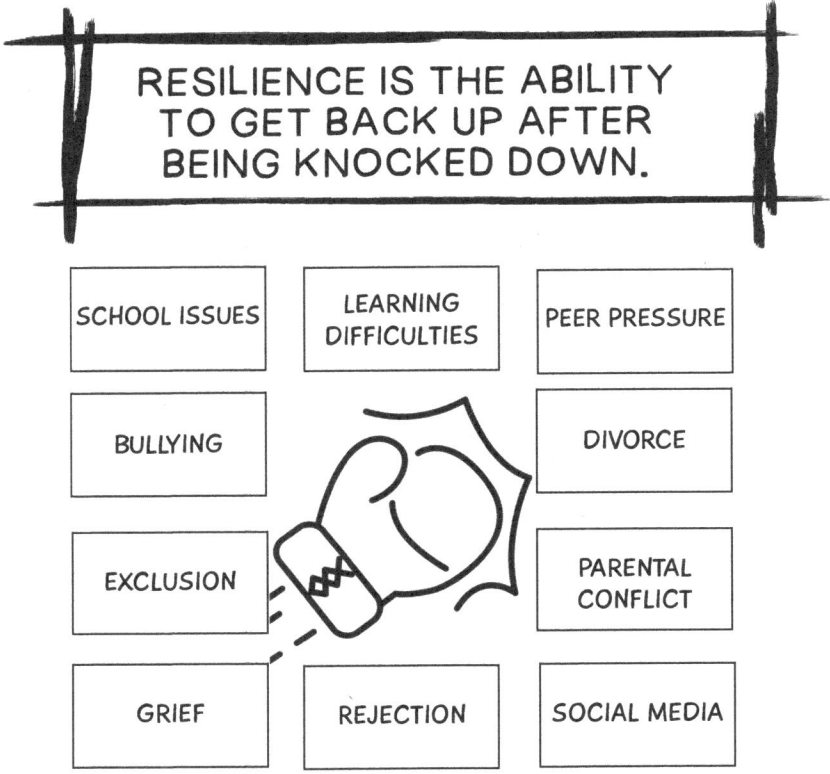

RESILIENCE IS THE ABILITY TO GET BACK UP AFTER BEING KNOCKED DOWN.

SCHOOL ISSUES

LEARNING DIFFICULTIES

PEER PRESSURE

BULLYING

DIVORCE

EXCLUSION

PARENTAL CONFLICT

GRIEF

REJECTION

SOCIAL MEDIA

These knock-downs our kids may experience include a wide range of life events such as:

- School issues
- Learning difficulties
- Peer pressure or 'butting heads' with peers
- Social media
- Exclusion
- Bullying
- Not getting picked for the sports team
- Grief

◀ Divorce

◀ ... (Insert your own experience here because the range of possibilities is never-ending).

I work with these struggling kids and teens every single day. Sadly, there are times – as with Mark – when life becomes too much. For many others, they're often walking a tightrope contemplating whether it's worthwhile opening their eyes to another new day.

Raising resilient children is not about the things we teach our kids and teens through what we say. It's about practical things that we as parents can do and change in our homes, starting TODAY!

It's that one-degree thing.

FOR BUSY, WORKING PARENTS

I hear you and I get it. If you're thinking you can't possibly fit even one more thing in your day, don't give up. The good news is that building resilience doesn't have to take hours every day. It's the little things that you can do that won't add to the bandwidth. You have the potential to make a profound difference in your child's life and when I, a fellow crazy-busy parent, remind myself of that truth, I breathe a MASSIVE sigh of relief.

Resilience, Attachment and Connection

Centred in the core of resilience lies the concept of attachment; our brains are wired, pre-birth, to attach to our caregivers. This wiring forms the basis of every aspect of our lives and provides the foundation for how we relate to others. It plays a significant role in developing resilience (of course!), our beliefs, our self-awareness and the development of empathy, conscience and compassion.

A caregiver develops a healthily attached relationship with their infant when they are able to consistently meet both their physical *and* emotional needs. This first relationship sets the foundation for all future relationships and, when it's a healthy one, it results in an adult who is self-confident, trusting, positive and manages conflict well. These adults generally also navigate intimate relationships, express and share their emotions with ease and ask for help and support without feeling threatened (or as if they are a burden).

In other words, these are the kind of adults we want our kids to become. But for many reasons (often ones that are outside of a parent's control) a healthy attachment relationship doesn't always develop and little – or sometimes enormous – cracks begin to form.

WHY HEALTHY ATTACHMENT RELATIONSHIPS BETWEEN PARENTS AND CHILDREN DON'T ALWAYS DEVELOP

Read this a few times: These reasons may be beyond a parent's ability to control. Leave the guilt at the door. Guilt only contaminates our relationship with our child and results in us trying to compensate in various ways — more often than not in unhealthy ways. So leave it all right here and move on without the 'G' word, please! You did the best you could with the emotional and physical resources you had at the time. A healthy attachment relationship between a caregiver and a child forms the basis for all other attachment relationships that the child establishes throughout their lives. When we consider that attachment wiring develops when a child's physical and emotional needs are met, we can see why the scenarios below may result in attachment difficulties.

These are just some of the many reasons why attachment relationships may be impacted:

◁ Physical and emotional neglect of a child

◁ Traumatic experiences

◁ Separation from primary caregiver

◁ Changes in primary caregiving

◁ Frequent moves or foster-care placements

◁ Primary caregiver's depression

- Maternal addiction to alcohol or drugs
- Undiagnosed painful illnesses — colic, ear infections etc. (pain is a barrier to connection)
- A parent's chronic illness
- Young or inexperienced parent with poor parenting skills
- Conflict within the home
- Inconsistent caregiving
- Primary caregiver's emotional instability
- Benign neglect.

We all want our children to develop happy and healthy relationships with us and with all the important people in their lives. It's essential to start at the beginning in this regard and to understand the importance of the *first step* towards resilience.

Bruce Perry, an American psychiatrist and a senior fellow of the Child Trauma Academy in Houston, Texas, and adjunct professor of Psychiatry and Behavioral Sciences at the Feinberg School of Medicine in Chicago, has done some groundbreaking work in trauma and resilience. He also has decades of experience in brain science, child development and trauma. Perry developed a hierarchy of the six core strengths essential for a strong childhood foundation for future health, happiness and productivity. Each one of these strengths, together known as the 'Vaccine Against Violence', develops sequentially and becomes the foundation for the next.

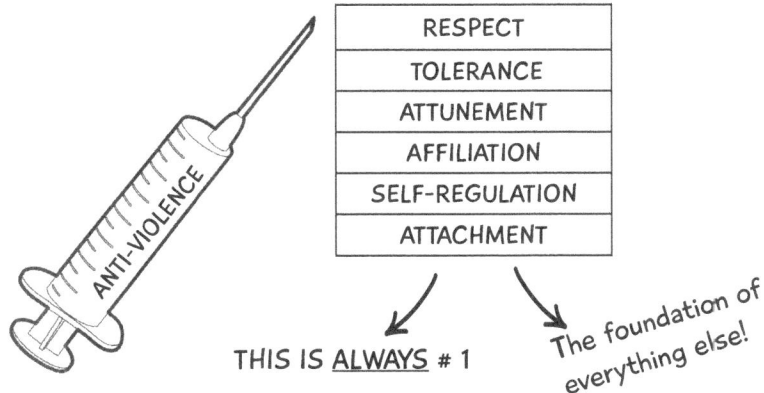

RESPECT
TOLERANCE
ATTUNEMENT
AFFILIATION
SELF-REGULATION
ATTACHMENT

ANTI-VIOLENCE

THIS IS <u>ALWAYS</u> # 1

The foundation of everything else!

Healthy attachment is the NUMBER-ONE priority.

It is the foundation of ALL other skills and it's the perfect catalyst for self-regulation, affiliation, attunement,* tolerance and respect. So often we expect all these other skills from our children and even punish them when we see them lacking, yet we are not concentrating on what's at the heart of it all and ultimately our primary focus – attachment.

 *Attunement: How reactive and in tune we are with another person's emotional needs and the space they are in. The process by which we form relationships, involving being truly present in the moment.

The next time you hear someone yelling at a child or teen, 'You have no respect!' consider whether that child has received the basis of a good attachment. When you're wondering why youth are often so intolerant of one another – be it on a cultural, racial or any kind of level – ask yourself if the majority of kids today ever had the opportunity to develop healthy, secure attachments. You'll soon discover the sobering truth that many of them have (sadly) not.

We need to reframe what we think we know and what we've

been taught and shift the focus to what our most important goal with our children should be. When you look at the research it's a no-brainer: attachment, attachment, attachment.

Maybe you're panicking to yourself and thinking that because things went wrong in your own life as an infant, or in your child's life when they were younger, that it's too late. It is most definitely not! Naturally, the earlier we build these healthy relationships the easier life is going to be for many reasons, but it's never too late to repair and rebuild. In fact, repairing and rebuilding with our kids and teens is essential and healing. Dealing with mistakes in a healthy way is so important in building resilience that Attribute 20 (discussed later in the book) is dedicated to this exact topic.

Because of our neurological wiring, relationships are the biggest buffers to life stress. Here's where the attachment comes in. Our mammalian human brains give us the same message all the time. `Relationships + togetherness + connection = safety`

In connected relationships we feel safe in an unpredictable and ever-changing world. Often the predictability of connection with a safe and trusted 'other' IS our only security.

For empowerment and resilience to develop, connection should be the number-one priority. Connection within the context of healthy relationships is our children's number-one defence against stress, depression and anxiety.

How to Get the Most Out of This Book

THIS WAY

What follows are 20 short, simple, yet hugely powerful ideas that you can begin implementing immediately. They will make a remarkable difference to how connected your child feels to you, how valued and worthy they feel and ... *drum roll* ... how resilient they become.

Studies show that if you read this book in one sitting, you'll likely only remember three of its ideas. I'd really like you to remember more. Read just one attribute, or even just one subsection, a day and mull over it. Think about what you need to change or how you can do things differently. Maybe you already have some of these mastered, in which case tick that box, but don't skip chapters. Our brains tend to remember (and perfect) skills the more we see them. That's the key: dip in when you need to and try them out in your home.

COCOON CONTEMPLATION MOMENTS

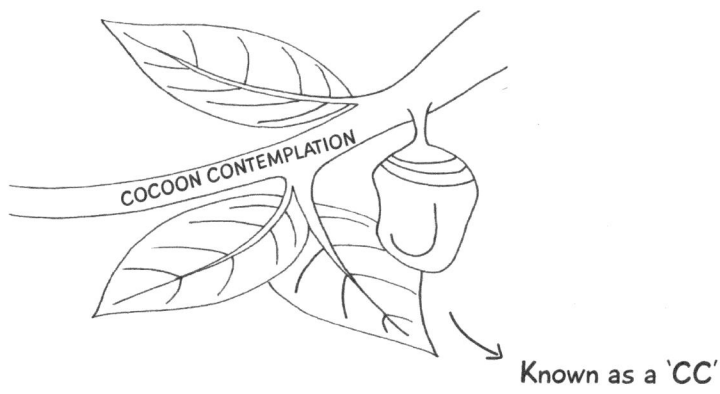

COCOON CONTEMPLATION

Known as a 'CC'

I am going to encourage you to take Cocoon Contemplation (CC) moments throughout the book. The thinking behind this concept is that during the time spent inside a cocoon, a metamorphosis is taking place. There's a brief retreat, an introspection, a pause in a safe, quiet space while some very important changes are happening. Transformation cannot occur without this pause and the reflective thoughts that follow.

Real earth-shifting, destination-altering change requires more than the 'a-ha' moments we have in our heads. They happen in the pauses, reflections and quiet contemplations (in the CCs) we have *after* the 'a-ha' moments. You're reading this book because you want change and the likelihood of that increases significantly when you make space for the CCs. After your introspective pauses, take a moment to write these reflections down. I encourage you to use the grey shaded blocks, the book margins or your own notebook for these; our thoughts and silent contemplations are powerful.

In case you're tempted to give 'jotting down' reflective moments in this book a miss, please don't. As a book enthusiast myself, I completely understand that writing in a book may be a hard mindset change — an uncomfortable one. I tend to treat books with a sacred respect, but just this once I encourage you to try inking (or pencilling) these pages, or jotting things down in your own notebook if you prefer. Really make this an interactive journey of learning and reflection. Acknowledgement is the first step to change and isn't that why you picked this book up in the first place? You want to make changes to best equip your children for life so get writing!

CCs are the bridge-building between the change we want and the change that is right there waiting to happen. The positive impact that these changes will have in your home and most importantly, in your relationship with your child, is the core take-home lesson.

Are you ready ... ?

PS These things have very little to do with your kids. They're about you – reframing your powerful role in this whole parenting process. So (as the old adage goes), without any further ado, here are the 20 attributes of PARENTS who raise resilient children.

PART 2

20 Attributes of Parents Who Raise Resilient Children

≈ Attribute 1 ≈

PARENTS OF RESILIENT CHILDREN … ARE RESILIENT

To get you into how things are going to work, we are beginning with a really short attribute. Just because it's short and less for you to digest it doesn't mean you should skim over it quickly. This is an important one. Really important. If we don't get this one right, and it's not an area we are constantly working on, the other 19 attributes really don't matter that much.

This can be a tough pill to swallow, but here's the fundamental reminder about all the qualities we want for our children: We cannot expect our kids to be anything that we are *not*.

I often have parents say things along the lines of 'Naomi, my child has self-esteem issues,' or 'My child has confidence issues. You need to work on that with them.'

My default response is always, 'What is *your* self-esteem like?' and 'How confident are *you*?'

Another common 'demand' I hear on repeat in my practice is 'My child has anger issues. You need to sort this out.' Then while I'm interacting with the said child during play therapy or psychotherapy sessions, they'll tell me something like, 'My dad came home last night and he slammed the door, kicked the dog ... (insert relevant aggressive act).'

Our children learn from what's around them. They learn from us and we are their 'life textbooks', their role models. Who we are, what we say to ourselves and others, and how we respond to situations determines how our children's brains are moulded.

YOU need to strive to be all those beautiful qualities that make up resilience before you can expect them from your child.

This is your first CC Moment right here.

 CC Moment: If you feel lacking in the resilience department, use that as your starting point because the rest is futile if you don't begin there. This is your number-one priority. Everything else will fall flat like a poorly baked soufflé if you don't start with you. Take a few minutes and write down what you need to work on.

 REMINDER: Our kids don't learn from what we verbally try to teach them. They won't learn resilience from any fancy-looking resilience programme that costs you a limb. Our children are copycats and they learn from us every single day — from the day they're born into this world.

If you remember one line from this attribute, let it be this:

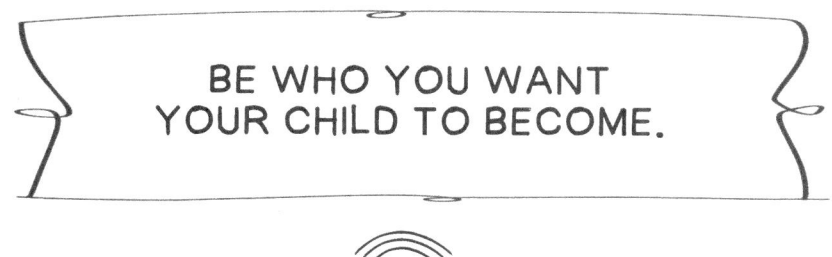

BE WHO YOU WANT
YOUR CHILD TO BECOME.

≋ Attribute 2 ≋

PARENTS OF RESILIENT CHILDREN ... PRIORITISE THEMSELVES

You may be thinking but isn't parenting about prioritising our children? It is, but here's why prioritising yourself *first* is essential. Our natural instinct is to put everyone and their needy requests (whether it's sandwich-snack-making, Lego-piece-hunting or lost-sock-finding right this minute) ahead of ourselves. When it comes to parenting we tend to make sure everyone else is okay and has all *their* needs met long before we consider ourselves.

Our kids are learning how they should value and treat themselves from us.

Let that settle in.

Another important **CC Moment:** Think over what you are teaching your children in terms of valuing yourself and jot some thoughts down on the page.

'The relationship you
have with yourself
sets the tone for every
other relationship
you have.'
ROBERT HOLDEN

This quote beautifully sums up why it is so important to prioritise yourself. There is no way to escape from this. When I run parenting courses or a series that lasts more than one week, often one of the homework tasks I'll give to participating parents is a self-care challenge. I tell them that for every day of the next week they need to set aside a short amount of time and do something that fills their soul. I'm asking you to do the same. And while we know how important exercise is, it doesn't have to be exercise! Maybe it's a walk in the garden, doing some painting, having coffee with a friend, hugging your dog or listening to a podcast. Do what fills you.

If leaping for self-care opportunities isn't your strong point (don't worry, you're not alone in this), have a look at the list on the next page and see whether any of these ideas speak to you. Then commit to trying out just one thing a day just for you.

- ✔ Walk around the garden barefoot.
- ✔ Throw a ball to your faithful hound.
- ✔ Call a soul-friend.
- ✔ Drink lots of filtered water daily (believe it or not, this counts as self-care).
- ✔ Hit the gym or put on your running shoes and hit the road.
- ✔ Head to the mountains, go for a hike, take deep breaths and get that fresh air into your lungs.
- ✔ Find a quiet corner and cry it out (from a neurological perspective, crying is healing and definitely counts as an act of self-love).
- ✔ Enjoy a candle-lit bubble bath.
- ✔ Read one chapter of that book that's been sitting on your bedside table for months.
- ✔ Try out rebounding (a mini trampoline exercise — it's my daily sanity 'go-to'!).
- ✔ Head out to a kid-free dinner with your partner or even by yourself.
- ✔ Breathe! Quite simply, just sit still and move any electronics or distractions away from you. Take five deep and slow breaths. It is a straightforward yet nourishing exercise that is so often overlooked and yet it is healing and full of self-care benefits.

'BUT I FEEL SO GUILTY!'

When the guilt of taking time for myself starts sneaking up on me, to get some perspective I ask myself: 'When am I my best self?'

Being my best self enables me to be the best parent I can be for my kids. For me, it's my rebounding session every day, a quiet cup of tea in my office garden and writing blogs and books. This is how I 'give back' to myself so that I can (as far as possible) stay in tune with my kids' emotional needs when I am with them.

Whatever filling your soul means for you, do THAT every day for one week.

When I ask the parents on my parenting courses how their week went after taking even just ten minutes every day for themselves, the response is usually something like, 'My relationship with my kids was so much better. I wasn't as impatient,' or 'Even my relationship with my partner has improved.'

This is because *all* the people around us benefit from the time, care and self-love we pour into ourselves. As a parent you have to reframe yourself as a fuel tank that your family is 'filling up' from all the time. If you aren't filling yourself up, not only will you not be able to show up for your kids, meet their emotional needs and be tuned into them, but you're likely to become easily dysregulated and cause greater disconnection in your relationships. Remember that in order to build resilience, we need maximum *connection*.

If the thought of *any* time for yourself sends you on the 'selfish bus' (we're talking about more than hiding from your kids for 15 minutes behind a locked bathroom door with a slab of chocolate), remember that self-care is the kindest and most important thing you can do for everyone in your family.

 What have you done for yourself lately? Or, more accurately, what have you done for yourself lately that helps you show up and be more in tune with your kids? When it's put that way, it kind of changes the importance of the question, doesn't it?

Here's a one-week challenge for you to commit to. Do it for yourself. Do it for your children.

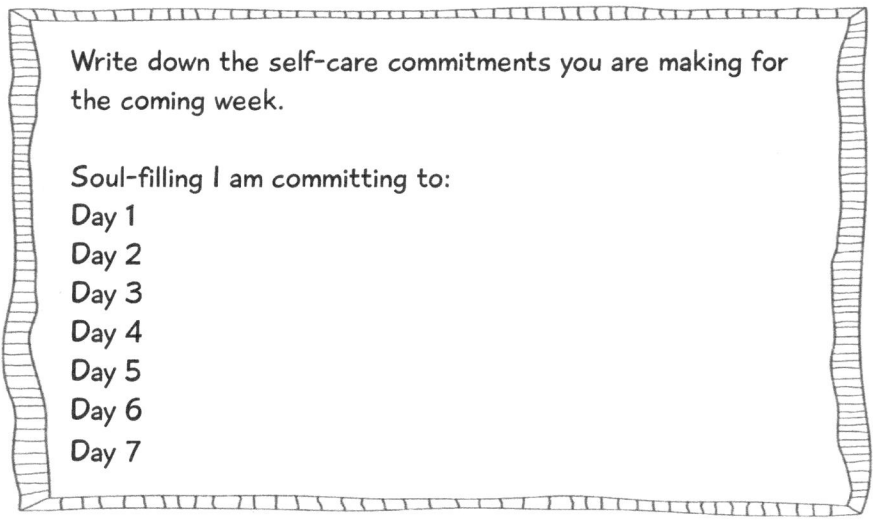

Write down the self-care commitments you are making for the coming week.

Soul-filling I am committing to:
Day 1
Day 2
Day 3
Day 4
Day 5
Day 6
Day 7

After one week ask yourself the following two questions (this is definitely a CC Moment):

 How do I feel?
Has this had a positive influence on my family?

If you need an extra push and some 'hard-core' evidence as to how imperative self-care and reduced stress are when it comes to parenting, let me leave you with the outcome of a study that was conducted by Ellen Galinsky of the Families and Work Institute in the United States, a research organisation that focuses on family and the workplace. She did a survey of 1000 children and asked them, 'If you were granted one wish about your parents, what would it be?'

Guess what their answers were? The kids' number-one wish was that their parents would be less tired and less stressed. The takeaway from this? Sleep more and make stress reduction an essential part of your everyday life.

We cannot expect to raise resilient kids if we're not looking after ourselves and placing our own self-care high up on our list of priorities. Even from a neurological perspective, in order to be resilient, we *need* to practise self-care. Once we start falling by the wayside when it comes to taking care of ourselves (and I don't mean your daily shower and brushing your teeth!), we tend to snap more easily, we become less immune to overwhelm and we end up just being 'less nice' humans all round. It **MUST** begin with us.

GETTING SERIOUS ABOUT SLEEP

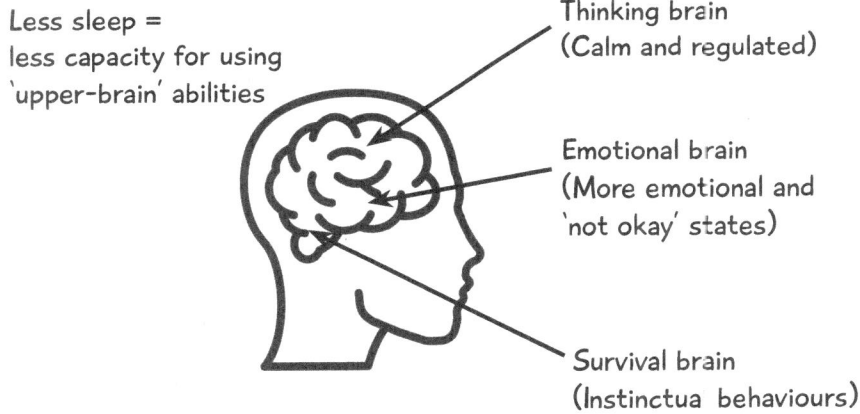

Less sleep = less capacity for using 'upper-brain' abilities

Thinking brain
(Calm and regulated)

Emotional brain
(More emotional and 'not okay' states)

Survival brain
(Instinctua behaviours)

I firmly believe that one of the foundations of good parenting is getting good-quality sleep. It's common knowledge that adequate sleep is the foundation for ensuring good health, but how do parenting + sleep go hand in hand?

So much is happening in our brains when we don't get good-quality sleep. Our chances of falling into the 'limbic state' of functioning (dysregulation) increase and in the limbic ('not okay' and more emotional) state, we end up walking a fine line between tiptoeing along the edge of a cliff and landing in the pit of dysregulation.

It goes without saying that none of us are at our best if we haven't slept or we're lacking proper sleep. We're prone to being more crabby, edgy, less patient, moody and our irritability levels are at unhealthy levels. When we haven't slept enough our responses/reactions to our children's needs lean towards the irrational.

One of the best things you can do for yourself and your loved ones in this regard is to acknowledge the things that steal sleep time from you (think binge-watching the latest series on TV or scrolling aimlessly on your phone) and make an effort to replace these lost hours with precious, restorative sleep hours. Charge your cellphone away from your bed and invest in some light night reading for when you may not be able to get back to sleep. Reading a book makes it much easier to fall asleep compared to looking at a screen and the associated blue light (which lessens the production of melatonin).

How much sleep is enough?

Here's a rough guide not just for your kids, but for you too! The right amount of sleep makes it far more likely that everyone in the family remains in a regulated state.

1–2 years old	11–14 hours per 24 hours plus naps
3–5 years old	10–13 hours per 24 hours plus naps
6–12 years old	9–12 hours per 24 hours
13–18 years old	8–10 hours per 24 hours
Adults	7 or more hours per 24 hours

 REMINDER: Dysregulation leads to disconnection. To build resilience our aim is always connection. (I repeat this phrase throughout the book because it really is **THAT** important!)

Self-love is the first step in taking care of yourself so that you can take care of others. If you think back to the last few times that you lost it or clashed with your kids and teens, in order to stay grounded and breathe through it, you would have needed to be in a regulated state. In the absence of self-love and self-care you *will* be triggered more often. GUARANTEED! If you're not looking after yourself, regulation is going to be a mammoth task.

 What do the words 'regulated' and 'dysregulated' actually mean?

There's an incorrect assumption that the word 'regulated' means to be calm, but it is broader than that. Regulated means to be in control of our physical responses and emotional state relating to what's happening in our environment at the time. 'In control of' are the key words. You can be hugely excited, i.e. far from being calm, in relation to something incredible happening in your environment and still be in control of your emotions, i.e. you can still be regulated.

The term 'dysregulated' is when we are, for any reason, unable to control our emotional responses and our energy levels aren't suited to the 'goings-on' in our environment. The key words are 'out of control', which is, of course, a disempowering space for anyone to be in.

 REMINDER: It's not just children who struggle with dysregulation, many adults do too.

≋ Attribute 3 ≋

PARENTS OF RESILIENT CHILDREN ... KNOW HOW TO
BREATHE

When I say 'breathe', I definitely don't mean the normal
breathing we do involuntarily!

Whether you are a mom or a dad, whether you had a natural

birth or a caesarean section, whether you attended any pre-birth baby classes, you would have been taught how to breathe during the imminent time of the baby's arrival. Whether we physically attend classes or read glossy baby magazines, we all learn about the 'breathing technique' *before* our kids are born. We're taught how to breathe *before* that little human makes their appearance in this world in order to help us reduce pain *while* they are making their appearance. But does anyone actually tell us that one of THE most critical skills in parenting that we will require beyond 'post-kid' arrival until our kids are 18, 20, 30, 40 ... actually, *always*, from that moment onwards, is breathing?!

Breathing is the how-to-urgently-regulate-myself-and-calm-down-right-now life skill that's essential for a plethora of reasons. The unconscious in-and-out breaths that you don't think about yet take daily (roughly 22,000 times in 24 hours) aren't helpful when it comes to regulation and whenever we are triggered or our heart rate increases for any reason, the number of breaths we take increases. We need to slooooow things down to stay regulated.

We can't parent properly if we can't (consciously) breathe properly. Why? Because challenging things happen all the time and our kids *will* test us. Removing the ability to get those deep breaths in and out means you'll start feeling a little bit stressed and dysregulated. This applies to kids and parents alike. The emotional volcano starts bubbling up and erupts all over everyone in the near vicinity, causing complete carnage.

Once our stress hormones are activated (as so often happens when our children's behaviour triggers us), the fastest way to bring our bodies back to homeostasis so that we can *respond* and not *react*, connect and not disconnect, is conscious breathing. It's the most natural thing we have at our immediate disposal, yet in times of dysregulation, when we are in the thick of a meltdown, it becomes one of the hardest things to remember. At that moment all we're thinking is 'Whoa! Rapid heart rate! Shallow breathing! Completely flustered!'

The more we understand about what happens when we are in a stressed state, the more empowered we are when it comes to making changes and the more compassionate we can be to ourselves and others. The neuro info below will hopefully help you to understand how imperative breathing is for you and your child's survival and sanity and the strength of your relationship.

GETTING INTO THE BRAIN

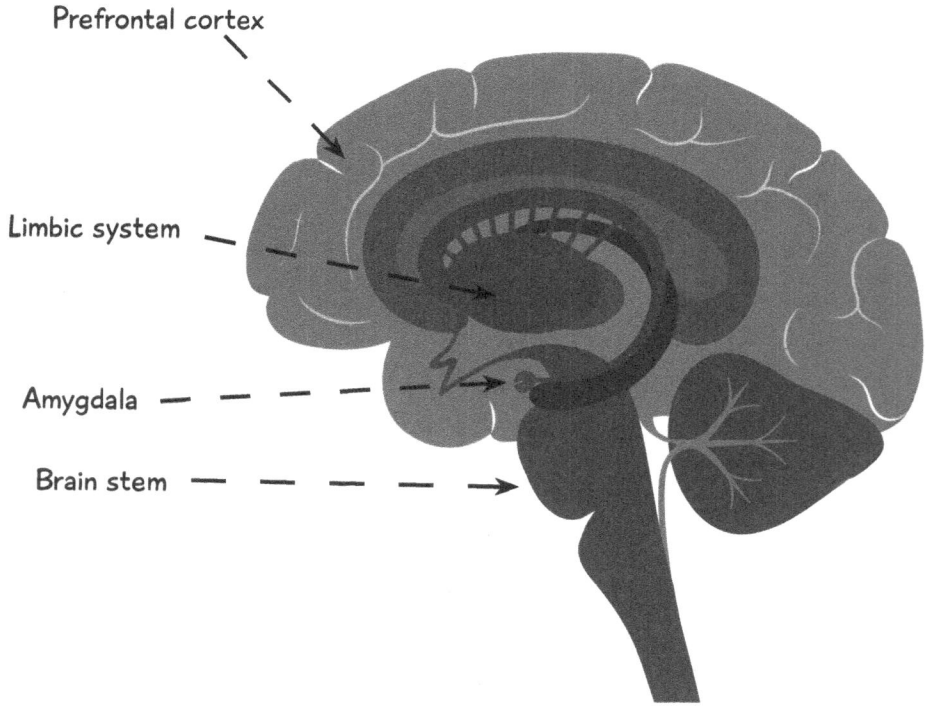

Prefrontal cortex

Limbic system

Amygdala

Brain stem

Here is the simple version of a very complex process that happens in the human body and brain whenever we are stressed.

A stress message is received via our senses and transported through the thalamus to the amygdala (I like to call this part of the brain its 'panic-button centre'). The brain then goes into full survival mode and neurotransmitters such as adrenaline, noradrenaline and cortisol are released. These flood the body and a cascade of remarkable things happen.

Firstly, our sympathetic nervous system is triggered. If you've heard about 'fight or flight', this is the state you'll find yourself in. You'll feel hot, strong and ready for some kind of action, either to attack or put on those roller skates and get the heck out of there.

Part of the process to ensure your ability to stay alive is that all the blood leaves the areas of your body where it is not immediately needed, such as your mouth and your digestive system. This is why in times of stress you often experience a parched, tongue-sticking-to-the-roof-of-your-mouth feeling and a sore stomach. There is reduced blood flow to those areas because most of the blood has swiftly run to the large muscle groups that are needed during fight or flight modes.

The brain's function at this point becomes single-minded: to keep you alive. To have the best possible chance of doing this, it cuts off the 'thinking' part – the prefrontal cortex.* It does this because if, for example, you were being chased by a lion, but you stopped to *think* about what to do, if you paused to assess which tree you should climb, there's a good chance you would become lunch for a very large and hungry carnivorous beast.

*Prefrontal cortex: This frontal-lobe region in the brain is implicated in executive functions such as planning, reasoning, problem-solving, impulse control, decision-making and working memory. It is also responsible for personality formation, moderating social behaviour and controlling certain aspects of speech and language.

Prefrontal cortex
(All executive-functioning skills) cut off

Amygdala triggered

Release of stress hormones into the body

Sympathetic nervous system activated

This doesn't mean there are no thoughts going through your mind at the time; you're just unconsciously 'doing' to keep your heart beating for the unforeseeable future. It's not only lions chasing you or other real life-threatening events that kick the brain and body into this state of nervous-system dysregulation. Whenever the brain detects something that may for any reason cause us to feel unsafe, that 'panic button' is activated. If you're not aware *when* that button is pushed and the 'red mist' starts rising, there's likely to be an explosion of epic proportions.

We may not realise it, but the following modern-life examples can lead to the same stress response unfolding in our brains as a life-threatening situation.

Stressors may include:

◀ You're stuck in traffic.

◀ Your computer crashes.

◀ You're late to fetch your child from sport/school/crèche.

- You burnt the rice/roast/potatoes.
- An email from your boss lands in your inbox demanding an urgent report.
- The dog ran through the house and traipsed mud everywhere.
- Your child ran through the house and traipsed mud everywhere.
- Your tween rolled their eyes, slammed their bedroom door and sent some serious attitude your way.
- Your toddler threw their spaghetti on the floor, pulled the cat's tail and ran away from you, or they grabbed tins off the shelves in the middle of the grocery store.
- Your teen sauntered in beyond their curfew, swore at you, told you they hated you and point-blank refused to study for their science test.

Some of these triggers may seem insignificant to you, but because all of our nervous systems are wired differently, an event that may seem innocuous to you may just trigger overwhelming dysregulation in someone else.

For example, the sound of a child crying is a huge stressor to many people and has been shown to cause the cascade of physiological processes in a caregiver that leads to their own dysregulation in a situation where they need to be as calm as possible. It is possible to master this automatic response so that outcomes can be better for everyone.

Your child and teen have their own triggers. Things that you may not find stressful can throw their nervous systems into complete dysregulation and have their brains believing that they are unsafe and need protecting at all costs. This sequence of internal events is all happening unconsciously and automatically. Of course, for a mature and developed brain, in a calm and rational state, it's obvious that not being able to use a spoon to eat your spaghetti, not getting what you wanted for dinner, having an annoying parent on your case or being late for school are NOT life-and-death situations requiring our bodies to go into survival mode. However, once any of us have been triggered, the brain cannot tell the difference between real and perceived threat.

A child whose sympathetic nervous system has been activated may display behaviour such as meltdowns, tantrums, hyperactivity and excessive silliness. This is *not* a naughty child. THIS IS A SIGN OF A BODY AND BRAIN THAT ARE DISCONNECTED, of a nervous system that is dysregulated and a little human being who feels unsafe. In a dysregulated teen who feels 'unsafe', behaviour may include excessive crying, unjustified anger, physical aggression towards themselves or others, rapidly changing roller-coaster moods and extremely high levels of anxiety.

It is for all these reasons that understanding what triggers us is essential. We *will* be triggered (more so if we're not following through on self-care and not doing the 'couch work'*) and one of these triggers *will* be our child/children. As tempting as it is, there is simply no point in yelling at your child in these moments because you'll both be in a state of alarm and dysregulation and your brain AND body will be screaming in unison: 'I am feeling unsafe!'

 *Couch work: The self-reflective and healing inner work we do on ourselves.

There's another layer in the survival system that is not uncommon for children to go into as fighting back or fleeing are often not viable options for them given their smaller size and strength. This state is explained by the polyvagal theory – formulated by Stephen Porges in 1994. Porges was the director of the Brain-Body Center at the University of Illinois in Chicago and the polyvagal theory that revolutionised our understanding of the states engaged by the brain during times of stress and trauma. This next layer of the survival system is one that's useful to understand because it's easily misinterpreted and overlooked.

When the brain perceives that being in fight-or-flight mode is *still* rendering the body completely helpless and disempowered and it feels unable to survive a situation, it heads into a state of freeze, faint or fawn. During this state of complete overwhelm, the dorsal branch of the vagus nerve in the brain is stimulated. This stimulation results in immobilisation and the child may then shut down, collapse or freeze. This is the brain's final attempt to keep our bodies alive. It's important to note that this state is often misinterpreted as complete compliance when it is actually complete overwhelm. In children and teens it could look like:

- Trying to please in order to avoid conflict
- Keeping quiet and 'flying under the radar' in homes where there are domestic disputes or abuse
- Slumped shoulders
- Withdrawal
- Extreme shyness.

In any state of nervous-system dysregulation, in order to find calm and feel safe again (meaning you will be able to show up as your best parenting self so that your kids can remain content, easy to be with and not drive you up the wall), we need to activate the state of social engagement in the parasympathetic nervous system. This is where the good stuff happens and is the zone where the ventral vagal nerve supports connection and engagement. It's the state in which we feel safe and it is the perfect condition to encourage creative play, curiosity, communication, learning and healthy relationships. When these things are happening, resilience is being built.

IN THROUGH THE NOSE, OUT THROUGH THE MOUTH

By now you can likely see the importance of conscious breathing. Every day most of us feel tossed into varying states of stress in this super-sped-up hamster-wheel-on-steroids journey of life, and because of this, conscious breathing (deep, 'regain control' breathing) is my sanity!

Here are three quick and easy breathing techniques that I teach my patients and my own kids and use myself (especially when I'm stuck in traffic). Make sticky notes of these and plaster them on the fridge as easy-access reminders when you encounter those really challenging moments in life and in parenting.

STRAW BREATHING

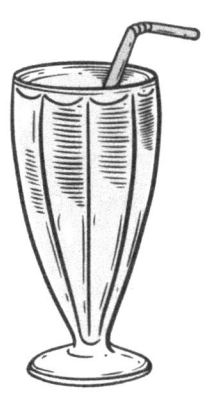

Imagine you are a kid again (it's really good to get out of our 'adult zones' sometimes so try to make time to connect with your inner child) and you're at your favourite restaurant and you have the biggest (insert your favourite flavour) milkshake in front of you. Take a two-count breath in through your nose and blow long, slow bubbles out through those straw-enveloped lips for four counts. The trick is that you need to breathe out for double the counts you breathe in. (Personally, depending on how stressed I feel, I either do a ratio of 2:4 or 4:8.) Try this breathing technique at least four times BEFORE you react to whatever triggering situation you may find yourself in.

Proactive regulation hack:
Start becoming aware of when you start to feel a little frazzled by detecting any signs your body may be sending you. Is your heart rate increasing? Are your cheeks feeling a little flushed? Do you feel a little hotter and physically stronger? Are your eyeballs glazing over with a red mist? All of these are signs that your temperature gauge is increasing and you need to run to the fridge and seek the advice of a trusty sticky note (and while you're there perhaps stick your face inside said fridge to cool down).

BOX BREATHING

I also call this 'four-square breathing' and it's a powerful tool. During a presentation on childhood anxiety, in an auditorium of a few hundred adults, I demonstrated this technique and by the time we were done, I could have heard a pin drop in that space. That is how incredibly calming and regulating this exercise is.

Picture a square. Once you can see the square in your head, you are going to follow the instructions over the page four times (look at the picture and try it):

1. Take a deep, slow breath in through your nose to the count of four.
2. Hold for four counts. (The hold part is really important and it's the step we often skip. Don't skip it! HOLD!)
3. Exhale slowly for four counts.
4. Hold for four counts again.
5. Repeat these four steps four times.

Tracing the lines of the square helps and you can practise it anywhere and teach it to your kids. If your home is anything like mine, no one is exempt from needing to practise some serious self-regulation techniques!

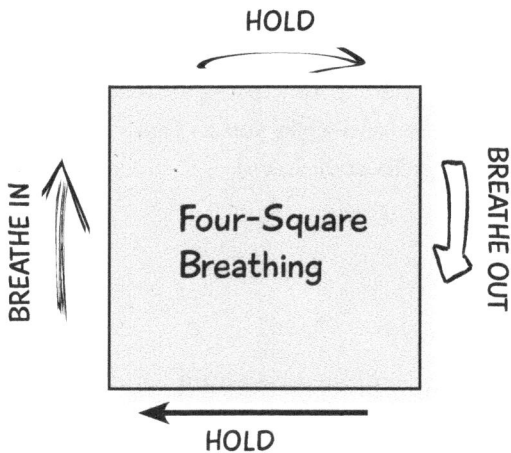

HAND BREATHING OR FINGER BREATHING

This is a good one to teach your younger kids or to use yourself when you're about to lose your rag at the dinner table.

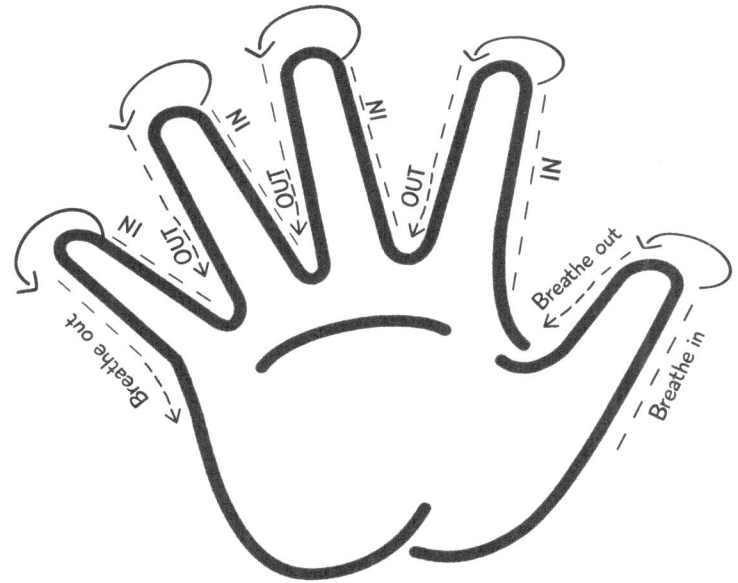

Follow these directions (if you are at a table, move your hands underneath it):

1. Spread the fingers of one hand.
2. Use the index finger of your other hand and place it at the bottom of your thumb.
3. Start tracing around the outer edges of the fingers from your spread-out hand, one at a time.
4. As you move your index finger upwards along your thumb, breathe in slowly and deeply.
5. As you reach the top curve of your thumb, start exhaling.
6. At the inner bottom of your thumb begin inhaling again as you start tracing your index finger in an upward direction.
7. Keep tracing the outline of your hand. In ... out ... in ... out ...

By the time you get to the end of your pinkie finger you should be feeling a WHOLE lot more regulated, calm and ready to tackle whatever is happening at that dinner table.

BACK TO THE BASICS

There are going to be plenty of times you're going to flunk the entire 'self-regulation' exercise, which is perfectly okay because you're human (and I've dedicated a whole attribute to maximising our fallible human selves to the benefit of connection with our children), but the good news is that practice makes perfect. The more you do it the easier it becomes to remember the technique when you're smack in the middle of one of those heated moments.

Every time we practise *any* new skills (including the parenting ones), the wiring in our brains that helps us to automatically remember these skills becomes just a touch stronger.

But no matter how strong the wiring gets, unless you are a Tibetan monk with 60 years of meditation experience, you remain fallible to normal human stress responses. The good news is that NO human being on this planet can be regulated 100% of the time (not even the said Tibetan monk is immune so toss that parenting guilt out the back door).

Another point to remember that may feel a bit strange, but can really help, is to proactively practise breathing. By this I mean not just waiting until the 'red-hot chilli' moments happen to wonder what the heck you are supposed to do and how you are supposed to do it. Practise in the calm. When you're gardening, while driving (sans road rage), when you're walking the dog, while you're washing the dishes, sipping tea or having your favourite treat, practise breathing techniques. The stronger that wiring becomes the easier it is to jump on to that brain pathway during those 'hotter' moments. When we're able to breathe through those moments there is a much lower chance that we're going to react and cause a disconnection.

The aim is to add as many **CONNECTION** moments as possible to your day. If these breathing practices can help you do that then you are on the right path and by doing this you are helping your child build *their* resilience.

◈ Attribute 4 ◈

PARENTS OF RESILIENT CHILDREN … ARE BRAVE ENOUGH TO LOOK IN THE PARENTING MIRROR

Have you ever wondered why your children behave so foully, give you the most horrible attitude and are generally up the wall and off the rails on days when things have gone pear-shaped in your life? Maybe the pipe burst, the printer jammed, your boss called you in at 4:55pm and requested an 'urgent' three-hour analysis report, you had to get the cat to the vet for an emergency hairball incident, your major client is considering signing with another service provider or supplier … Just an average crazy day including any, or all, of the above (or any similar crises).

On days like these you may find that your children's somewhat 'off' behaviour is just adding to the mammoth stress you've already had to endure. You may even find your internal dialogue to your children is along the lines of: 'Of all days, why did you have to choose

TODAY to behave like a feral creature?'

The answer is not what we want to know or hear. Brace yourself.

It's because our children are mirroring us.

One of the powerful and most difficult things I've had to learn to do as a parent is when my kids are being off-the-wall, I take a deep breath and ask myself, 'What is going on within ME right now that could be impacting, causing or resulting in what's happening in front of me?'

This journey of reflection is not an easy one, but it *is* an essential one. When your children and teens behave in ways that you don't understand, or they show any signs of being unkind, sulky, whiny, or really anything that classifies their behaviour as 'difficult', the first place to start looking is in the parenting mirror.

Too many parents are too scared to stand in front of that proverbial parenting mirror and ask, 'What's going on *within* me?' It takes bravery and courage, but when we're able to do this we are less likely to react to the behaviour our children are displaying and more likely to respond in a manner that will maintain CONNECTION (yip, there it is again, the incredibly important 'C' word).

Your kids' behaviour could be caused by a range of issues that we can't even begin to go into, but this is a book about YOU and what YOU can do so let's stick to focusing on the really empowering YOU stuff.

From a neurological perspective, your child is absorbing EVERYTHING around them. All your non-verbals, your stress levels, your tone of voice, your body language, those loud and heavy sighs; those little sponges that are our kids are absorbing ALL of it. This is causing heightened arousal in their sensory systems and they are going to be dysregulated if we show we are (in any way) *not* okay.

Work sits somewhere near the top when it comes to my triggers. There is a direct correlation between when I'm feeling stressed, when there's a deadline looming, when a talk I'm presenting needs prepping and how I then react to normal, developmentally appropriate child behaviour. When I am stressed, that normally appropriate behaviour can sometimes feel too much for me to cope with not because it is, but because I am dysregulated for a reason completely unrelated to my kids.

The response from most parents I've asked about what their biggest trigger is has been the same: 'My trigger is work.'

 CC Moment: When are you triggered and more likely to react to your child's behaviour?

I recall a recent single-parenting week some time ago (one of those weeks when, naturally, the parenting load doubles and things generally flounder somewhat when only half the workforce is on hand). I was scheduled to deliver an online talk in the evening but we were in the throes of load shedding* and it had been one of those days when everything that could go wrong did go wrong.

 *Load shedding: A frequent scheduled 'pause' — of around two to six hours — in South Africa's electricity supply in order to reduce pressure on the country's electricity generators.

I had 20 minutes before starting a presentation and I was still making last.minute.com PowerPoint adjustments. My kids were playing outside and I asked them to finish up and come in so I could get them fed and ready for bed. They were taking their sweet time, as kids who don't have our concept of urgency do.

Feeling just a little frustrated, I stomped outside to frog-march them into the house. As we came inside my daughter said to me, 'Mom, I thought rebounding was supposed to make you happier.'

I had to have a good chuckle to myself because even *she* knew that self-care is essential.

The way we react to our children is dependent on our emotional space, not on what they are doing ... or what they're *not* doing. (Ironically, I had done a rebounding session that morning or who knows how I would have responded in that moment.)

When I'm triggered and stressed, I know that there is NO WAY I can be completely in tune with my kids and their needs. None of us can fully show up for our kids when we're in this state. When I start to feel the beginnings of wanting to lose my rag with my kids' behaviour, I stop myself before I react. I haul out that mirror and have an internal chat with myself and tell myself that my kids are likely just being kids. This is not about *their* behaviour. It is work that is triggering me *not* my kids.

If I don't do that, I'm going to (unfairly) take it out on them. When I manage to do the mirror work, I'm able to tell myself to stop, take a breath and remind myself this is about *me* and *my* stress. Instead of snapping, I can ask them in a calm and measured tone to either stop the behaviour or take it elsewhere. (Very often whatever they are doing that is causing that 'red mist' to rise in me is just absolutely developmentally appropriate childhood behaviour that my dysregulated state is struggling to process. Asking them to continue with it elsewhere is often the best thing to do.)

DOING THE INNER WORK

I don't believe that any of us have ever fully 'arrived'. We are never fully healed. Healing is a continuous journey and we're walking this path all the time. All of us are learning, all the time. Whole children have *healing* parents. Our constant focus, every day, needs to be consistently working on ourselves and our healing.

BREAKING THE CYCLE

From the first moment we hold our newborns in our arms and look at those beautiful, perfect eyes peering back at us, many of us vow that we will *never* do some of the things that our parents did to us. We will *never* parent like we were parented. Despite these intentions, we frequently fall into these patterns unconsciously. It's often in a parenting moment that we realise that we are mirroring exactly what our parents did to us and exactly what we *didn't* want to do to our children. It's in these moments that we often realise hard things about ourselves, our parenting *and* our parents.

The reality is that if we do not actively head out on our own self-healing journey and figure out what the emotional 'trash' that we've been handed actually consists of, and what we need to work on moving and changing within ourselves, all that happens is that we keep passing that trash bag on. Even with the best intentions, it's our wiring and it's our default. We are neurologically wired from the youngest age to repeat patterns that were role-modelled to us. We parent the way *we* were parented.

It's not intentional, but it is ingrained beyond our control. The good news is that just by acknowledging what we need to change, we are already taking steps towards doing this.

From the moment they are born, you are growing your child's brain through your every verbal and non-verbal behaviour. Who *you* are determines how your child's brain is wired and how it develops through your everyday actions in and towards the world.

It is imperative that we do the couch work and change our wiring so that we can offer our children a better future. This takes a huge amount of introspection and difficult mirror work, but it is the most liberating experience to be able to look at your children and say to yourself, 'I've set you free from a cycle of intergenerational trauma'. We *can* do the couch work and free our children from these cycles.

> 'WE ARE PRODUCTS OF OUR PAST EXPERIENCE, BUT WE DON'T NEED TO BE PRISONERS OF IT.'
> Rick Warren

How would you describe yourself?

Let your internal voice do the talking and write a paragraph in the box below.

Write down the things you like about yourself as a person, as a parent, as a partner and an employee or business owner.

Write down the things you wish you could change about yourself – things you don't like, perhaps parts of you that you try to hide.

Write down some of the thoughts you have about yourself and your abilities as you go through your day. Do you tend to be harsh and self-critical or are you able to be compassionate with yourself?

_____

_____

_____

_____

_____

_____

_____

_____

Now for the **CC Moment:** How much of what you wrote down was positive?

This exercise is meant to help you relook at the way you talk to yourself and recognise the power of your internal voice. We become who that internal voice tells us we are and we can't expect our children to be anything that we are not or cannot be. We can't expect our children to absorb the positive about themselves if we aren't able to do the same. Our children are mirrors and sponges and absorb, reflect and observe everything about the people we are. We need to aim to be who we want our children to be and treat ourselves with the kindness and compassion that we want them to treat themselves with. If our inner voice doesn't align with our wishes for our children, that's the part we need to begin working with.

I often think of some of the teens I have worked with who suffered from eating disorders and said things to me like, 'I remember how my mom would look at herself in the mirror. How she made comments about how her butt looked in her jeans or how unhappy she was with her appearance.' Or 'I felt really hurt when my mom saw a lady walk in front of our car and said, "Look how she let herself go." If she can judge other people like that, I know she's judging me too.'

The way boys see their moms looking at and treating themselves is how they learn to one day treat the women in their life. And how dads treat moms also teaches boys how to treat their future spouses. Dads' relationships with their sons and daughters have exactly the same impact in terms of teaching them how they should treat others and be treated in relationships.

Too often as parents we put ourselves and others around us down.

Big CC Moment: Our kids and teens are watching and learning from everything we do. The positive and the negative. The affirming and the critical. The compliment and the insult.

THE IMPORTANCE OF CONSCIOUS AWARENESS

If this all feels like too much pressure, too much information and too much to take in, the important thing to remember is that conscious awareness changes everything. The conscious awareness you will have gained *just* by reading this book will help you feel empowered and I hope will help you realise that the smallest recognition can make the biggest difference.

The first step to change is not going to be sitting down and planning *how* you're going to do it; the first step to changing anything in life, whether it's a relationship, work or any aspect of life, is acknowledgement of where change needs to happen.

If you catch yourself sometimes 'losing the battle' to stay regulated don't be so hard on yourself. Don't berate yourself with words like 'failure'. Show yourself some compassion, be kind to yourself and remember that we are all continually learning and healing. Gently remind yourself that recognising it is exactly how we change it. *That's* how we change our wiring.

We don't need a magical tool. We don't need luck. We just need to acknowledge and, through acknowledgement and active reflection, we can change the wiring. This is where your CCs come in *really* handy!

> We as parents do the couch work so that
> our children don't have to.

This doesn't necessarily mean that the couch work has to be with a psychologist once a week. It's simply the acknowledgement of the things that we want differently for our kids and *how* we want to raise them differently. It's the CC moments (and the introspection that goes hand in hand with these) that result in conscious changes being made within ourselves, for our children.

'RUNNING THE HARD YARDS'

Many of you had amazing role models in your parents and that has made a profound difference in your life and how you turned out as an adult. For others (me included), maybe you want to work on certain aspects of yourself that have been a direct result of a 'not too wonderful' childhood. When we don't work on these, they can contribute towards laying the perfect foundation for depression and anxiety in our children. I know that, as far as possible, I want my children to have a life free of these.

Their dad and I need to *be* the change to create the change for them.

It goes without saying that this is hard work, but it is comforting to know just how possible it is through the simple act of conscious awareness and the harder act of constant self-work.

Knowing all of this means we are equipped and able to change things for our kids. I look at my kids every day and remind myself that I'm changing the cycle for them. By breaking an intergenerational cycle I'm giving them the most powerful gift. As parents we have the potential to change generations of harmful, disconnected and even abusive parenting by choosing to say:

'It stops with me.'

⪡ Attribute 5 ⪢

Let me first say that if you're a single parent, I take off ALL the hats I own to you. Single parenting is unbelievably challenging – doing it alone, day in and day out, physically, emotionally and in every other way possible.

I see you and I acknowledge you. You are incredible and most certainly capable of raising resilient kids and teens.

It's important to remember that family structure can take many forms. Family is that feeling of 'home', no matter where that is or how many people it's made up of. More on this later.

If you are in a long-term partnership, take a moment to imagine the scenario that most often happens. These new little humans take centre stage the minute they enter our lives. They are our suns, our moons and all the stars in between. They are the centre of our solar system and inevitably we (along with our partners) revolve solely around them. But it is in this process that we often move further and further apart from one another. Our little darling/s stay in the middle and the radius of the orbit gets bigger and bigger until we wake up one day and our partners are light years away from us. We hardly know them any more because – understandably – it's ALL been about the kids. We sometimes reach a point where even thinking back to how we connected in the first place or how the relationship was is near impossible. A bit like the paddling-inside-a-washing-machine effect.*

 *Paddling-inside-a-washing-machine effect: The chaotic busyness of everyday life and the desperate attempts to keep afloat through it that result in us feeling like we've been spun through a few cycles in a washing machine (upside down, back to front and soap-sudded).

> If you're married or in a partnership,
> have you been on a date night in the last month?

When I pose this question to a live audience there are usually just a few hands that very hesitantly go up. Sometimes none go up at all.

> Have you been on a parenting weekend
> or holiday without your kids lately?

As for this response, I hardly ever get any hands raised.

I completely get it. In our busyness of everyday life, we often just don't prioritise quality time alone with our partners. There are so many other to-do items that fall above date nights and couple weekends and many parents who don't have extra family support find it extremely challenging to secure reliable and trusted caregivers for the time they're off playing 'couples retreat'.

But creative problem-solving when it comes to finding babysitters is so important. In a two-parent household, a significant degree of our child's sense of safety and stability and of who they are in this world comes from the perceived degree of stability of our relationships with our partners. It's important for your children to see that you are connecting as a couple, that you actually enjoy being in each other's company and can even have fun together.

Do you know what usually happens on a couples' weekend? For the first 24 hours the only thing you talk about with your partner is ... you guessed it ... the kids! And then you wake up the next day and start chatting again and usually that's when an 'awakening' of sorts settles in. When you remember, '*That's* why I chose you. I actually *do* like you' or 'Now I remember why I proposed to you! You really are more than just my children's mother (or father!)'

We forget because our identities become so rooted around one thing and one thing only – our role as parents. Our sense of self in this situation is easy to forget and kids need parents who know who they are and can – where possible – experience the benefits of a strong, connected relationship between their parents.

It's so easy to lose connection in our marital or long-term relationships. There are days we are so exhausted that the last thing we feel like doing is interacting meaningfully with the other adult in the house, and once those kids are in bed we head straight for that pillow or Netflix series. It takes a decision, commitment, practice and a willingness to grow to reconnect with our partners.

Set aside time to remember *who* you are married to or in a

relationship with and consciously work towards reigniting that connection (or keeping it alive). Being a parent is the greatest honour in the world, but for the mental health of your kids and teens it's vitally important that they can see that you are a parent PLUS a human being in a loving relationship. Here are some out-of-the-box date-night ideas to try:

✔ Have an under-the-stars picnic.
✔ Head to a local art gallery.
✔ Sign up for a dance class.
✔ Play a few rounds of Mexican Trains (google it!).
✔ Join a cooking class.
✔ Go on a wine-tasting.
✔ Go to a show or a music festival (just buy those tickets, dress up and get out there).

So often I hear parents say, 'We have no support crew (aka baby-sitters) and date nights just can't be done,' so here are some ideas of things you can do together in the comfort of your own home! Choose one of these and then get creative with your own ideas:

✔ Join a virtual scavenger hunt (google it if you're not sure!).
✔ Do couples yoga on the lounge floor.
✔ Make home-made pizza together over a bottle of wine.
✔ Plan your dream holiday together.
✔ Have a pillow fight.
✔ Dress up and turn your lounge into a dance floor. (If the kids are sleeping, use earphones.)

- ✓ Get out the Scrabble, UNO or Monopoly and have a games night.
- ✓ Look through your years of photos and reminisce together.
- ✓ Recreate your first date at home (if possible).

Hopefully one of these suggestions will spark an idea that's possibly already spinning around in your head. The main thing is to just DO IT. Your connection with your partner will make a significant difference to your children and to their sense of belonging in a loving family system.

╾ Attribute 6 ╾

PARENTS OF RESILIENT CHILDREN ... KNOW THE VALUE OF INVOLVED FATHERS

If you're a dad, I'm pretty sure that your commitment to spending hours reading a parenting book means there's a reasonably good chance that you are *already* an involved father.

If you want some reassurance that you are doing the right thing by being involved, research tells us that children who have involved fathers:

✔ Have higher social skills
✔ Display greater confidence
✔ Have more self-control
✔ Are less likely to engage in risky behaviours in adolescence
✔ Show more self-discipline
✔ Do better at school (Yes! Even this!)

The bottom line is that involved fathers impact in countless ways on the lives of their children and on the people that their children become. Despite this, there is still an archaic version of the role of a father in a child's life and usually the version includes: Dad goes to work, Mom takes the lead on the cooking and cleaning, Mom does the homework with the kids and Dad comes home exhausted after a hard day at the office, just in time to say goodnight to bathed and fed kids!

In my practice, in the masterclasses that I host, the parenting courses I run and on the social media pages I follow, there has been a huge shift in how dads' roles are changing. Dads are actively recognising the need to be involved in their kids' lives and realising the significant impact that their involvement has on them. Ultimately, both father and child experience joy within these deeply connected relationships.

A father's involvement is where we begin to make changes in this world. Our children need dads who pay attention because that's where so much of their sense of self comes from. We know how important moms are, but dads traditionally tend to leave the 'little everyday bits' up to the moms. The nitty-gritty of parenting, the nappy changes, the dropping off at parties, the making of school lunches, checking the sports kit is packed for the next day – those 'invisible' things that happen without anyone even noticing. BUT guess where the connection is built? In those nitty-gritty, not-always-so-pleasant times of parenting.

To all you moms, why this happens also needs to be mentioned. Too often *we* are the ones who deprive dads of carrying out the 'mundane' tasks because we believe that in some way we're better at doing them.

Mom watching Dad attempt to change a nappy:
'No, no, no! You're doing it all wrong. Just let me do it.'

Mom watching Dad supervising the bathing:
'Their faces are still dirty. Look at that mud on their feet! Just let me do it!'

I'm the first to admit that when my son was a newborn, my children's father was more 'in the know' about nappy changes and bathing than I was and I had to stand back and learn. Having two younger siblings, he got to watch and learn the process of 'raising babies'. I, being the youngest of five, had slightly less experience in this area. (He insisted that I add this in and, while it's absolutely true in my case, I know it's definitely not the norm in most households!)

When we as moms take away the moments in which we feel we could do things better, quicker, or because our kids prefer the way we do it, we are taking away opportunities that hold potential for the greatest connections.

It's okay if the nappy goes on backwards. Yes, there may be some spillage, but in the greater scheme of things connection and bonding in those moments are more important. And it'll only take one 'poopy incident' for the nappy lesson to be well learnt! It's okay if your child's hair isn't brushed perfectly or if a slightly muddy smear remains on their ankle after dad's been in charge of bath time. What's more important is that kids know their dad is in their life. That they know their dad cares enough to get messy and be a part of the mundane grittiness of the 'everyday' realities.

That is what speaks value to them.

 Some time ago, I read some very sad statistics that said most dads only spend seven minutes PER WEEK of real connected time with their children. That's devastating and if our children are meant to be getting so much of their sense of importance, value and esteem from the time dads spend with them, it's not a good sign for our next adult generation's mental health.

But it's not just a lack of time from dads. Our lives as moms are also frantic and sometimes I don't think we do much better. If you think about what connected time actually means, it means putting all else aside (including your phone), stopping that hamster wheel of life and paying attention.

We need to get into our child's world and stop expecting them to get into ours before we can connect. At times, during therapy sessions with parents, I will ask, 'When do you spend time with your child?' The response is often something like, 'We've got an hour trip in the car to school in the mornings,' or 'They come with me when I play golf or when I go to the gym.'

This isn't 'connected time' in their world. This is us taking them alongside in *our* world. As wholesome as these experiences and memories can be, what brings far more value to their lives is when we as adults get out of our 'adult world' and take the time to find out how to step into theirs with no expectations. *That* is when we experience the depth and beauty of real human connection. *That* is when our children feel *truly* valued and loved.

Attribute 7

PARENTS OF RESILIENT CHILDREN ... CAN PUT CONSISTENT
BOUNDARIES IN PLACE

This is a hard one. We are all busy parents so consistency is challenging, especially when we are exhausted at the end of a long day. But the thing is that the greater the storm (and undeniably the world has experienced some huge storms over the past few years), the more the need for the safety and security of boundaries. Kids feel safe within boundaries – boundaries that don't move or change on a daily basis. If you set a boundary today and tomorrow it shifts, or it shifts when you are too tired to stick to that boundary, the change causes your child to feel insecure.

Let's begin with a basic understanding of what is meant by 'boundaries'. Boundaries are a set of values that are learnt and understood by all family members that are needed for the well-being of all. In my practice one of the most common things parents want clarity on and help with is boundaries. Often they walk out of my office or when the Zoom session ends saying something like, 'Oh, but we actually knew this stuff and it makes so much sense.' About a week later I'll usually get a call to say that things are so much better at home. But then about a month or two later I'll get another call to say, 'We need to come and see you again. The wheels have come off.'

Within five minutes of the second session, most parents are glancing at one another either with a knowing nod or an under-the-breath comment like 'It's the boundaries!' Turns out they actually didn't need to come back to my office; they really just needed to go back to the basics of consistently parenting with clear value-based guidelines that each member of the family is well aware of.

The issue is that when we shift the boundaries, things go wrong. Not because our children start misbehaving, but because they begin to feel insecure. A child who doesn't feel secure and safe is a child who becomes dysregulated. As I've said before, behaviour is a message. Their message here is loud and clear: I don't feel safe. I need the consistency of boundaries.

Think about your house as an example. If you're living in a country other than South Africa you may not have the security measures that we have, but try to visualise it anyway.

Imagine that you are in your home, but your electric fence isn't working, the doors of your house have been removed to get fixed, the security alarm is faulty, your movement sensors are randomly going off and your security company is on strike. Plus, you've just received an urgent notification that the Five-Minute Gang* is in your area.

 *Five-Minute Gang: Crime syndicates who very efficiently gain entry and loot a house before making a quick escape within five minutes.

As an adult, how would this scenario make you feel? Would you put on a good movie, have some chamomile tea and then head to bed for a peaceful night's sleep? Or would you be at that front door waiting anxiously with whatever weapon (cricket bat, golf club, weighted mom-bag or whatever you can find) to protect your family?

No guesses for what your response would be ... You would be waiting ...

That is how it is with boundaries. When our kids don't know where the boundaries are, they don't feel safe enough to develop their self-esteem because they don't feel confident enough to just go out there knowing that within the boundary they are safe.

Independence doesn't develop from tossing our kids out into the big wide world and shouting, 'Run! Off you go! You'll figure it out!' It happens when they feel safe enough to grow away from us. Boundaries are required for this critical part of resilience – the ability to be independent of caregivers. Our kids need to know that they are safe. That they can move around. That they can grow and don't have to worry about the world outside those fence lines taking them down. That they can focus on being a child and develop confidently and safely.

 REMINDER: The more consistent the boundaries are the happier and more resilient our kids are.

In fact, we cannot have happy and resilient kids without them knowing where the boundaries are.

Maybe you have teens and feel this doesn't apply to you, that you are 'beyond' the boundary stage. To put this into perspective, a few years ago I saw a young adult – let's call him Peter – who had just come out of a drug rehabilitation centre. I asked him, 'Peter, if your parents could have done one thing differently, what would that have been?'

He replied, 'I wish my mom had said "no" more often.'

His words not mine.

Of course we might be putting up with our teenagers rolling their eyes and slamming doors, and perhaps even a few choice words that are tossed our way, but the interpretation of boundaries for our children and teens is 'My parents care enough'.

GENTLY SAYING NO

When any of us hear an adamant 'No!' in response to a request, there's a switch that flicks in our brains. We head into defensive mode. We feel a little offended. That 'red mist' rises and we shift off-centre a bit – maybe even becoming a little frustrated or irritated. Our kids are human too and every time they hear the word 'no' for any reason, that defensive 'red mode' kicks into place too! That doesn't mean we should take all boundaries down and always say 'Yes' to them (this will really only cause chaos and lead to disaster in our homes). It also doesn't mean that it's not important for them to ever hear the word 'no' – albeit gently (that's going to be a part of life that we want them to get used to within the safety of our homes). But thankfully there's another way ... We can say 'Yes' and still keep within the limits we have set.

Here are some practical scenarios (and while you are reading them, notice what reaction the word 'no' causes within you):

Scenario 1: Half an hour before dinner

Child: 'I want a cookie,' or 'Please may I have a cookie?'

Parent: 'No, we're eating in half an hour. No cookies before dinner.'

Result: Likely some kind of pushback, possible eye-rolls and an annoyed child who does not feel that you are fully understanding their need for a cookie. You may even have an emotional volcanic eruption on your hands or a complete dinner refusal.

Alternative: 'You can ABSOLUTELY have a cookie after dinner/tomorrow when you get home from school.'

You see what I did there? I didn't say 'No', but I still didn't allow my child a cookie at that moment. I said 'Yes' within acceptable limits for cookie-eating.

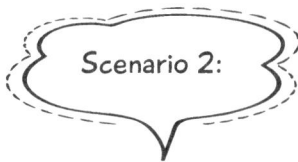

Scenario 2:

Teen: 'I really want the new iPhone.'

Parent: 'Not a chance! Do you know how much those things cost?!'

Alternative: 'You can absolutely have the new iPhone when you've saved enough money for it.'

Your child and teen aren't always going to respond without kicking up a fuss, but the survival instinct in their brain won't be triggered and you have so much more of a chance of retaining peace and connection (what we are always aiming for – *connection*) in your home.

Here's another consideration that has so much to do with one little word 'Don't'.

Read the sentence below and then close your eyes straight away and think about what you were visualising when you read it:

'*Don't* run through the house.'

What did you visualise?

I bet you imagined yourself or someone else running through the house! What we are doing when we use the word 'Don't' is actually reinforcing the exact behaviour we are wanting to discourage.

Alternative: Get the child's attention by using their name and, in a calm voice, reinforce what you do want: 'Frankie, we walk through the house.'

Now when you visualise that sentence, I bet you visualised walking and not running. It's a few simple word changes that have such power in what we are communicating to our children.

With small changes in the words we use, we end up reinforcing completely opposite behaviour.

Scenario 3:

Parent to a child having a sibling argument: 'Stop being so unkind!'

Alternative reinforcing positive: Use the child's name and speak in a calm and regulated voice:

'Meg, in this house we practise kindness towards one another.'

Again, you're not likely to see one child immediately apologising and running for a Sibling of the Year award, but you are reinforcing your family values in a positive way. You don't need to say anything more – just leave it at that. The reminder alone serves as a strong values boundary in which your child will feel safe.

Whenever you can say 'Yes' within boundaries, do it, and instead of reinforcing behaviour you would rather not see in your home, ditch the word 'Don't' and state what you *do* want to see more of. These small changes make a significant difference to what you are communicating to your child.

BEING THE BRAKES

Our children's brains are still developing and they continue to develop until their mid-20s. Certain prefrontal-cortex skills have not yet developed and so sometimes we need to *be* the brakes. This doesn't mean that our teens will like the boundaries or limits we set or that they won't question them. In fact, it's developmentally appropriate that they *do* question them. Your role at these times is to *really* listen to their perspective and ensure that even though you may disagree, they feel that you have understood. Sometimes, after hearing a teen's perspective, we may realise that we have set a limit that is unfair. In these moments, as parents, we need to be able to own our mistakes and be willing to change our minds.

The primary way that children and teens learn to set healthy limits and boundaries is by having parents who set them during their younger years. It can be challenging to know what limits to set with our teens. Always head back to values: Does what they are asking or how they are behaving align with our family values? Talk about these values often – at dinner time, during car rides – and make them a part of your daily conversations. When your child feels rooted in a sense of belonging in your family, and they feel as if their opinion matters and is being heard, you'll find you have a far easier time setting boundaries with them.

AN EXTRA REMINDER FOR PARENTS OF TEENS

If you are the parent of a teen, it's essential to remember that your teen's brain is still developing, and due to major 'reconstruction' going on with all their neurological wiring, they are not yet capable of making responsible decisions in all situations without your guidance.

You wouldn't give your child or your 18-year-old the keys to a sports car and tell them, 'Have fun out there!' We need to be the brakes. We need to be the clutch while they learn to change gears and while they are learning to pause before they act. This happens when we can empathetically and consistently hold the boundaries in place. When we are able to do this, a child's interpretation is that a parent who can put their foot down and tell them 'no' is also a parent who cares about them and can therefore protect them from the outside world and all the chaos that goes on in it.

UNDERSTANDING YOUR TWEEN AND TEEN'S BRAIN (IT'S NORMAL!)

The behaviour in your tweens and teens that drives you insane at times, and may even cause you to question whether you're raising a future convict, is *absolutely normal*. When we understand behaviour and what drives it, it's so much easier to be compassionate in those 'heated' moments.

Imagine a home that's undergoing MASSIVE renovations. There are builders everywhere – drilling, hammering, pulling down, tearing apart; it's loud and chaotic. There's cement dust on every surface, debris flying around and there's not one corner that's really comfortable to sit in. It's an absolute tumultuous upheaval.

That's pretty much exactly what's happening in the tween and teen brain. A complete overhaul.

It seems like it happens overnight. Just like that, our caring, kind, affectionate, considerate little people seem to become self-centred, argumentative, moody and inconsiderate.

Before you take it personally and wonder where on earth your loving darling has disappeared to, try to remember: THIS IS A NORMAL, HEALTHY, DEVELOPMENTALLY APPROPRIATE season of their lives. (And those 'hormones' that we are always so quick to blame actually only make up a very, very small part of the 'goings-on'.)

Your tween/teen's brain is beginning the remodelling stage that continues until roughly their mid-20s. It's doing exactly what it's meant to so that they can enter adulthood with a stronger, faster, more sophisticated brain.

Our children's role at this time is to begin to become independent from us. They NEED to push boundaries, to talk back, to argue, to pay more attention to peers, to throw some attitude (and possibly a few expletives) as a part of this season.

 Stop the panic!

This doesn't mean they've completely disregarded every value you have ever tried to instil in them. They're just figuring out how to begin living THEIR OWN lives. They're working out things that are important and valuable to them. As hard as this 'pushback' and change may feel to you, your tween/teen is learning critical life lessons here.

Naturally, your instinct may be to react. (Let's be real, honest humans here, this season can result in some hurting and confused parent-hearts.) What's so important is to remember that despite how their behaviour may seem, due to all the internal chaos happening (in the brain and everywhere else) your tween and teen need you more than ever. Let me repeat that: THEY SERIOUSLY NEED YOU.

They need you to be the trampoline on which they push back and test limits. This is how our children build autonomy – in the safety of our presence, knowing that no matter how hard they push, we will keep standing by and not abandon them.

This massive step towards independence isn't your tween rejecting you. Don't take the perceived rejection personally. It's really, really not. You're not going to want to hear this, but it's a much harder stage of life for them than it is for you as their parent.

If you want to be the parent your tween and teen most needs, here are two frequent messages I hear in my therapy room from kids in this season: 'I feel like my parents don't understand me' and 'I feel like they don't hear me.'

Make those your aims: Listen – without judgement or 'superior opinion' – and understand without reacting.

🏴 (Side note: I am not saying this falls anywhere in the 'easy-to-do' category.)

Let your home be the safe space in which they learn about standing up for themselves, in which they learn to have a voice, in which they learn that their opinion matters, in which they learn that whoever they may become during the remodelling, they are valuable and worthy of 'non-reactive', unconditional love.

It's your tweens' and teens' job to change. It's yours to remain consistent while their brains and bodies undergo reconstruction. When your focus is on your relationship with them and connection above all else during this season, in between the construction chaos, you're going to experience so many beautiful moments along the way and the end result of the unsettling remodelling is going to be absolutely breathtaking. (Mark this page and return to these words as often as you need to. I already know that this page in my personal copy of the book is going to be completely worn!)

THE PUNISHMENT VS DISCIPLINE DEBATE

There's often confusion around the concepts of punishment and discipline. When I use the word 'boundaries', I don't mean punishment. Somehow there is a warped idea that

```
boundaries = punishment
```

This couldn't be further from the truth. We desperately need to revisit what the word 'discipline' actually means.

Many of us were raised in homes where the basis of discipline was on the premise of religion and the 'Spare the rod, spoil the child' proverb. Interestingly, this is not from the Bible. It's not even close to a religious quote. It was written by an Englishman, Samuel Butler, in 1660, and appeared in his satirical poem entitled 'Hudibras'. Somewhere in history this proverb became distorted and churches clung to it, placing the fear of the wrath of God in congregants if they didn't practise corporal punishment within their homes.

 If you follow a Christian faith you might feel that perhaps I am treading on blasphemous territory. I encourage you to rethink this and have a CC Moment while you read the next few paragraphs.

If religion is the basis of the way you choose to parent, it's imperative to relook at what a shepherd's rod was actually intended to do: to protect the sheep, to rescue them, to keep them safe, to guide, to lead. A shepherd's rod was never, ever used to beat the sheep.

The word 'discipline' comes from the Latin word *disciplina*. It is derived from the root word *discere* which means to learn, to hear, to get to know ... NOT to beat.

Our job as parents, as we guide our children through life, is to *hear* them, get to *know* them and learn *who* they are. When we make that our primary focus and build a relationship with them based on security and connection, only then will our children be open to learning from us as role models. They'll become more open to listening to us as mentors and accepting our guidance throughout their life's journey.

_____
_____
_____
_____
_____
_____
_____
_____
_____
_____

The most effective way to build a brain is not by using harsh punishment. In fact, punishing a child causes their brain to become stuck in a vicious cycle of fear and survival. Learning cannot take place when we are in a state of fear and anger and are unable to access our prefrontal cortex properly. When we're shouting, yelling, raging or punishing, we aren't teaching our children anything other than role-modelling what a dysregulated adult looks like. By doing so, we are strengthening *their* wiring of how they demonstrate their dysregulation the next time they feel out of control. When a connected and attached relationship is present there is no need to parent using fear. Mutual respect, listening to one another and feeling understood happen within the context of a healthy parent-child relationship. Knowing what we know when it comes to the brain and how it functions, the most effective way to teach is to reflect and *be* everything you want your child to be.

 REMINDER: Our children become who we are and they earn through what we role-model.

BUT THEN HOW ON EARTH DO I DISCIPLINE MY CHILD?

This is when I usually, be it at parenting talks or in private consultations, get asked exasperated questions like, 'Naomi, how *should* I discipline my child?'

When it comes to discipline in our house, we don't base 'allowances of behaviour' within the confines of 'rules'. Rules don't work. Why? They create the potential for a fear-based hierarchy system that usually fails epically *and* they usually need to be changed every month or two once the poles of behaviour in the house shift. When you understand a child's behaviour from a developmental and emotional perspective, then you really don't need rules. You need a whole lot of patience and constant self-work so that regulating yourself becomes easier – but not rules.

 I believe in values that apply to every single being living under one roof and they're the same for every age bracket. In our home the one value that guides all behaviour is KINDNESS.

Unlike rules that need changing, none of us will ever outgrow this value.

Our kids' brains are physically developing through what they see role-modelled by us so if you want kind kids be a kind parent. That turns around our understanding of what is required in us as parents in order to 'discipline'. We are there to guide. *That* is our role.

One way that I constantly reinforce values in my home, and encourage introspection on these, is through using the 'three gates' as the guideline. I refer to them so much, in fact, that when I start repeating them my kids will often finish my sentences for me. These three questions form part of a quote by Rumi, the great Sufi poet.

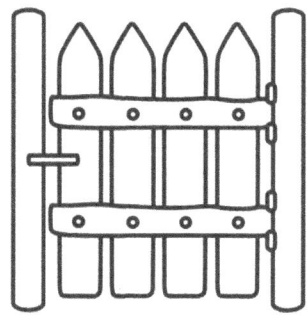

BEFORE YOU SPEAK,
LET YOUR WORDS
PASS THROUGH THREE GATES.

Although his quote refers to the words we say, in my home I have extended its use to guide our actions and behavioural responses to one another too. This doesn't just apply to my children's actions but also to my own. We hold one another accountable to following these guidelines.

This is what our three 'gates' look like:

 Is it kind?
Is it true?
Is it necessary?

Whatever is said or done in our house has to go through ALL three gates first.

Let's say my daughter asks how to spell a certain word (this happens often). My son may make a comment, 'How can you not know how to spell that?'

In a calm tone I ask him, 'Was that kind?'

'No, Mom.'

'Was it true?'

'Yes, she should know how to spell that word!'

'Was it necessary to make that comment?' (Although he may at first feel it was, when we have all had time to reflect on it he knows it wasn't.)

I remind both my children at this moment that in our house what we say and do cannot just pass through one or two gates. It has to pass through ALL three for it to align with our family values.

The conversations we have around these gates are powerful and end up being really reflective for everyone. And the added bonus is that when you are focusing on kindness, the natural by-product that develops is empathy. Win-win!

So when 'stuff' is going down in your home, here are the two questions to ask:

1. *Is this behaviour developmentally appropriate?* Most often, I can promise you it is. And on this note, our expectations of our children are too often to be 'mini adults'. They're not. They are kids. It is SO important to remember this in the 'hot' moments.

> Often, it's our expectations that need to change, not our children's behaviour.

2. *Is there something emotional going on in my child's world that they are trying to communicate to me?* Remember that children communicate using their behaviour. They're unlikely to pull you aside and ask for a chat to

tell you what's bothering them. The far greater likelihood is that they will behave horribly and you will be the recipient of that behaviour. I get that your first instinct is to react to that, but take a deep breath. First ask yourself the question 'What's going on for them?' This will enable you to have a whole lot more compassion and patience, and rethink the issue requiring 'discipline' entirely. But none of this is possible when you can't self-regulate and when your child's behaviour triggers an emotional state in you.

Two small phrases, 'self-care' and 'couch work', are key in helping us steer through this journey of life and appear throughout this book. Own these phrases and behaviours because they're the *only* way you get through the tough stuff. When things are heading south fast in your home, visualise a flashing neon sign that says:

IT'S NOT PERSONAL.

Behaviour is never personal. It's always just a message communicating a need and most often that need is connection. Try to remember that first and foremost and you will see behaviour changing. Once we understand that, it's easier to regulate *our* nervous system, and only when we have done that will our child's nervous system start to become more regulated.

When the fires are raging in a child of any age and the house is threatening to burn down, remember that a calm brain is needed to calm an uncalm brain.

The other critical factor is presence. We tend to send our kids away from us either through shouting at them or banishing them to their rooms in these fiery moments, but the brain learns regulation from being in the presence of a regulated 'other'.

NOTE: Asking a child to take their activities that threaten to derail us away to another location is different from sending them away from us when they are melting down.

We want our children to grow up to be regulated adults. We all know or have seen a dysregulated adult and it's not a pretty sight. So what's essential in these moments is that we try to be calm, regulated and remain with our child while the storm rages and eventually passes. (If they banish you from their room, stand right outside the door.) You can't see what's happening in their brains at this time, but little neurons are firing like crazy and regulation is being learnt. You may not see the fruits of your labour for a long time, but keep at it and you *will*.

 A last thought on the boundaries and 'discipline' issue: Life is not perfect. As human beings, we are not perfect and we cannot expect as much from ourselves or our children. It's a messy dance, but a beautiful one too. All that is required is for you to listen to the music and keep following the rhythm with your child. Remembering that imperfection is what life is about takes so much pressure off the parenting journey and enables us to enjoy so many more moments along the way.

PS There's a whole section on how to gently and compassionately put boundaries in place at the end of Part 3, for those parents who want more in terms of how to manage behaviour.

Attribute 8

PARENTS OF RESILIENT CHILDREN ... FOCUS ON
FOUNDATIONS

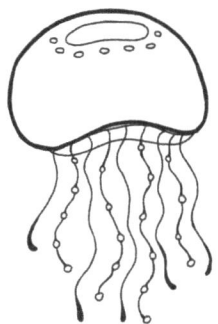

Far too often in my practice I see children who I call 'floaters'.
A 'floater' is not the visual that your mind is probably conjuring up right now! Instead, think of a buoyant jellyfish floating

aimlessly in the current. A 'floater' is a child who has a home, a family, goes to a good school, has all the bells and whistles that they may need, but has no sense of belonging. Because of this they have no idea who they are, they have no sense of identity and they lack resilience entirely. It is our roots that keep us grounded and stable through the strongest storms.

One of my favourite quotes is a Malaysian proverb that says:

'A TREE WITH STRONG ROOTS LAUGHS AT STORMS.'

We build these strong roots through the little things that we say, do and practise in our homes that are unique to our families, and that make our children proud to be a part of a family system. Little things that give our children ownership and that are often infused with fun and laughter too, all add to how much they feel they belong and WANT to belong to their 'clan'.

 What do you do in your home to grow strong roots? Think about the small family traditions that you have. Set aside a CC Moment here.

FAMILY TRADITIONS

In my home we do things like Friday-night boogey-downs, Friday home-made pizza or home-made burgers, Sunday-afternoon movies, birthday breakfast tables, dinnertime quizzes and a gratitude practice on the way to school in the mornings.

Maybe you do things like tea and biscuits in bed on a Sunday morning, dog walks in the evenings, or sharing a 'good part and bad part of the day' every night. Traditions are simply things that your family do together on a regular basis. They are what make you a cohesive unit and they are unique to your crew. There are almost limitless options for what these may be, but in families with traditions of any sort (no matter how small or seemingly insignificant), kids tend to feel so much more of a sense of belonging.

The storms in life are constant and we can't stop them, but when they come we want to know that our children's roots run deep and are strong. We want to rest assured that the tree representing their foundation will stay standing.

Resilience and a sense of belonging cannot be separated. I see this time and time again in my practice and within my own home. When children feel like they belong and are a part of something bigger than themselves, then there is no limit as to what they feel they are able to achieve and how loved and valuable they feel in the world.

Write down your family traditions in the box below or think of some that you are claiming for your family and going to try or implement from now on.

These traditions, which may not seem so important to us, leave our children feeling a sense of 'I belong here. I am a Smith, I am a Singh, I am a Ndlovu. I am a ...' Your children need to feel a sense of pride and a sense of belonging in who they are and in the family that they're from, no matter how unconventional that family may seem. They need that. It's these little things that your children are going to do with their kids and that are going to get passed down from generation to generation. These small 'extras' that are unique to your family are the things that make them feel rooted in a sense of family. It's within a sense of belonging that all human beings can thrive.

BECOMING 'BIGGER'

After decades of research by two psychologists at Emory University in the United States, a scale was developed to measure how much children know about their families. The 'Do You Know?' scale and its results highlighted that children who could answer 'Yes' to most of the questions exhibited higher levels of self-esteem, a greater sense of self-determination and fewer behavioural challenges.

Questions in this study included things such as:

- Do you know how your parents met?
- Do you know where some of your grandparents grew up?
- Do you know the source of your name?
- Do you know the names of the schools that your mom went to?
- Do you know which person in the family you act most like?

When children believe that who they are is 'bigger' than themselves, have a sense that their life didn't begin at their birth and won't end at their death, and they are part of a larger family structure, they feel more rooted, more of a sense of belonging and thus are naturally more resilient.

Tell your children stories about your childhood, your parents, weird relatives and odd places your ancestors may have come from. Research your family tree. Investigate if there were any criminals, explorers or famous inventors in your family's history. Tell them stories about things that matter to you from *your* childhood. These become the underpinnings of the roots we want them to be growing.

 A while ago something happened in our house that really brought home the importance of the rootedness and belonging that come from a sense of ancestry. My daughter's words to me that day were so precious and meaningful at the time that I wrote a short piece about it. It's called 'Hand-stitched with love'.

Two days ago, my little girl walked through the dining room with this ... A handmade, carefully hand-stitched, green material teddy bear. One that my mom had made for me in my early teen years. My daughter had dressed it up in her pink, glittery Build-A-Bear dress and she cradled it delicately.

I glanced at her and gently commented, 'You won't find a bear in the world that's more filled with love.'

You see, there's a story to that green bear.

I grew up as a preacher's kid in a home where some days, leftovers were a luxury. On rare occasions we received something new, but we certainly didn't get to 'submit' present lists of any sort for Christmases or birthdays and, most often, our gifts were handmade.

My mom would spend the year gathering and safekeeping all kinds of bits and pieces, and in the days preceding those special occasions, she would often work tirelessly into the early-morning hours to create something magical.

That festive season, in the midst of her war with cancer, my mom had carefully created this precious gift for me — each stitch, handmade, with love.

I remember the exact Christmas that this bear was wrapped under the tree.

I remember that all I had wanted that year was a kitten.

I remember feeling anger ... feeling disappointment ... and feeling let down as I ripped open that candy-cane wrapping paper.

Although I could not understand those raging emotions at the time, my wise mother did ... They were only the cries of disempowerment and helplessness from a young girl who somehow knew that her beloved mother was losing the battle.

Thirty-two years later, that green bear remains part of a precious and treasured memory.

After I had told my little girl the story of why no other bear in the world is filled with as much love, she held it even closer and replied, 'Mom, I think this bear of love should be in our family forever, and I should give it to my little girl one day ... and then she should give it to hers.'

Spontaneous warmth flooded my being ... 'I think that's a wonderful idea, my love.'

On that Christmas Day, a love so much greater than me had soothed my anger-riddled pain ... and now I carry that healing love deep in the veins of my soul.

And I remember ...

We don't pass down possessions

We don't pass down bank accounts

We don't pass down legacies

We pass down hand-stitched memories ... filled with love.

It's not the big things that we occasionally manage to do that give our children that sense of belonging. It's the mundane everyday things that often hold the key to the most powerful connection opportunities. It's the little things that are the most important, so don't put connection on hold for those big holidays and milestone events that you're planning for some time in the future. Know that connecting in the small family traditions and in the short pockets of time that you have each day can be some of the most powerful in helping your child feel understood, heard and grounded in a sense of family.

CHANGING PERSPECTIVE

For our kids, their perspective *is* their reality. In fact, that is the human truth for all of us. If you want to get really philosophical there is no such thing as reality. None. There is only perspective. There is your perspective and there is my perspective. When we are asking 'Does my child feel a sense of belonging?' and 'Does my child feel important in this family?' what we should rather be asking is 'What is my child's perspective of how valued they feel in this family?'

Too often it's the things that we don't recognise that are the most important to our children, not the big things. Those small, seemingly irrelevant things we say and do can have *the* biggest impact.

Maybe you are thinking, 'But we're saving up and in December we're going to Mauritius so we'll connect then' or 'We'll do something nice over the weekend after their sports match'.

I understand that overscheduled, working parent mindset of, 'I just can't. I *really* can't. I'm too stressed and busy'. But here's the thing: it's not only in those big holidays or fabulously planned events that meaningful connection happens. Our children perceive magic in so many of the things that we think are arbitrary. What's important is how *we* view those seemingly arbitrary moments and how we connect to our children in them. THAT's what makes their world special. (Teens are 100% included in this, by the way!)

 Big CC Moment: when you realise that you have to begin looking at the world through your child's eyes because that will change your perspective entirely.

When your little one is showing you snail shells, pay attention.

When your child is telling you about something their friend did on the playground, put down what you are doing and listen.

When your teen is fuming and cannot contain their frustration with the perceived unfair decision of a sports coach, empathise.

Read that extra bedtime story.

Cook their favourite meal just because.

Those are the things that matter.

Those are the things that ensure that they feel valued and worthwhile and rooted in belonging.

It's the smallest things that we pay attention to that have the biggest potential for connection with our children.

Attribute 9

PARENTS OF RESILIENT CHILDREN ... WELCOME 'BIG' EMOTIONS

(Just a heads-up: This is a long one because there are just SO many important aspects to cover!)

Many of us were raised in homes where emotions were ignored, swept under the carpet or where we were even punished for feeling them. Many of our parents could not tolerate our 'big' emotions, let alone know that what our brains needed for growth and to feel safe at those very overwhelming times was their presence and their unconditional love and acceptance of every single little and big emotion we displayed. I see this in so many of the kids and teens that I work with, and the truth is that I was raised in an environment like this too.

In homes where big emotions don't have a voice, the inevitable outcome is depression, anxiety and feelings of 'not being good enough'. Our kids and teens need to know that no matter what they are feeling or no matter what goes wrong in their lives, they can come to us. They need to see us as a safe space throughout their life. What too often happens is that big emotions are uncomfortable for us as adults and so we try to push them away and 'get through' them as quickly as possible.

Our unspoken message to our children always needs to be: 'I am not scared of your big feelings. Bring them on. All of who you are, and what you feel and experience, is safe with me'.

Too often when our kids and teens have those meltdown moments we tend to say things like:

'Oh my word. You're overreacting!'
'Not again!'
'Go to your room!'
(And many variations on the above ...)

None of these statements are really embracing or oozing with empathy. The hard truth is that the only reason that we can't sit in these turbulent spaces filled with overwhelming emotions is that we didn't have an adult to do this for us when we were children. When we are incapable of doing the 'sitting', the unconscious message we send our kids and teens is that emotions are 'bad', they are 'wrong' and that when we feel them we need to suppress them. But suppression leads to anger and depression. Processing life's big events and working through the traumas that we will inevitably face is in large part about being able to weave these into our stories of who we are and then being able to share them with the people we love.

I *want* to be that person for my children. I want to know that when things go wrong in their lives, they know that they can come to me. If they're not coming to me, it means they're going to their peers or to someone else, and there is no certainty about what guidance they will be given. Perhaps they are even trying to navigate whatever challenge they find themselves in all on their own without asking for support or guidance from anyone. This too could have dire consequences and be another fast-track to depression.

I have had plenty of exhausting days when I have sat on the landing with a sobbing and overwhelmed child on each leg without saying a word. All I have been able to focus on in these moments is regulating myself. I breathed and remembered those neon-flashing mantras, 'It's not personal!' and 'This will pass.' If you find yourself in these kinds of meltdown moments, breathe and repeat these mantras 100 times.

'GOOD' AND 'BAD' EMOTIONS?

We tend to classify emotions as good and bad or positive and negative. But ALL emotions are valid and normal. They are our body's interpretation of how it is experiencing our environment at a given time. Our emotions give us significant insight into how safe and comfortable we are feeling in our surroundings. When you're talking to your kids and teens about big feelings remember that every single emotion carries an important message and not one of them, especially anger, is a 'bad' emotion. (There's an entire section dedicated to anger as this poor emotion is given such a bad rap and is so often misunderstood!)

THE ESSENTIALS OF 'BIG' EMOTIONS

When your children are feeling any 'big' emotions and you are feeling triggered, remember the mantra (yes, again!) 'It's not personal!' None of the behaviours our children display or the emotions they show are personal. They are simply an indication of their emotional space and of their emotional needs.

When we are triggered by our children's emotional space, we tend to react to them, ignore them, or push their big emotions away. By doing that we are pushing our children away. Sometimes the last thing you want to do as a parent is sit in the space of a torrential meltdown or deal with an onslaught of volatile teen emotions, but it's exactly at these times that your children need you the most. In moments of overwhelming emotion we are all at our most vulnerable and what we need is a safe space to connect and regulate.

The ability to regulate our adult nervous systems is essential for healthy relationships and for general mental health. Without regulation, resilience is simply not possible because in times of dysregulation we feel overwhelmed and out of control. This leaves us feeling very disempowered. In this out-of-control and disempowered state, it's a much harder task to get back up after that 'knock-down'. This is true of any time when we are not feeling regulated.

Regulation is an upper-cortex skill in the brain and in an area (as I mentioned earlier) that is developing right up until the early adult years.

And here's the 'cracker' thing to remember.

Regulation cannot develop when a child does not have an adult who can co-regulate with them. The brain forms the wiring for regulation ONLY in the presence of a regulated other.

For most parents this is a huge realisation and needs lots of self-work. The only way to do it is to keep practising those breathing techniques and saying those mantras out loud. When our children are in those big, overwhelming spaces we need to be able to calm ourselves down first *before* we can show up for them and be right there in that messy, big, emotional pool they are wallowing in. We underestimate the power of simply being calm in this chaotic space of our children's emotional overwhelm. When we can do this we are sending some important messages such as:

'Your emotions don't scare me.'
'Your big feelings are normal.'
'I'll sit here with you through whatever you are going through.'
'Every part of you is acceptable and lovable to me.'

These words speak volumes to our kids about their worth. Our children can't process big emotions when they feel that those emotions are too big for *us* to tolerate. Instead of fearing the meltdowns, we need to reframe them and see them as the greatest opportunities for connection. It's in these moments of huge emotion that we as human beings are the most vulnerable and this allows the deepest connection to take place.

The dark spaces can feel unbearable, but there's a flip side – your child has come to you in their moment of greatest vulnerability. To YOU! At that time, what they need most is connection, not judgement, not scolding and not being sent away. Just you. You don't even have to say anything. All you need to do is to be able to hold the space for them. That's it.

BEING THE BIGGER BUCKET

When I use the term 'hold the space' when I talk to parents about what our children need in times of emotional overwhelm, I often get asked what I mean.

What our children need from us, no matter how old they are, when they are dysregulated for any reason (it's what human beings of *any* age need when we are feeling out of sync with ourselves and dysregulated), is to be able to 'hold the space'. Simply put, it is the ability to sit comfortably in the space of another person's uncomfortable emotions, while staying calm and regulated ourselves. It's key to try to befriend those emotions as the important messengers they are. When it comes to kids and teens, these emotions are what's giving you golden access to their inner world.

Let's imagine our kids' capacity to deal with emotions and big-life events as a bucket. Big-life events here are the ones *they* perceive as big, not you. For your toddler a 'big-life' event may be that they can't use their favourite cereal bowl at that moment because it's in the dishwasher; for your teen it may be that they have been blue-ticked by their current crush.

Little things that you may not even be aware of will start filling their bucket throughout the day.

For your toddler and preschooler, things that are 'big deals' may look something like:

- ◀ I wanted to wear my blue shorts, but Mom dressed me in green ones.
- ◀ I didn't want to eat cornflakes for breakfast, but that's what was in my bowl. I threw it on the floor to try to tell Mom that, but then she got really upset. I didn't know how else to tell her though.
- ◀ The dog jumped up on me and knocked me over.

◁ Dad wanted to brush my teeth, but he was going so fast because he kept saying he was going to be late for work. His voice made me feel a little worried.

◁ Mom put my school backpack on my back when we got to school, but it was too heavy.

◁ I couldn't take it any more and I needed to let them know that my sensory system was NOT feeling okay. I couldn't help what happened next and started having what Mom and Dad call a 'meltdown'.

For teens it may look like:

◁ My alarm went off this morning and I was still exhausted. I'm really not a morning person.

◁ I didn't have time to eat breakfast because Mom was stressing out about being late for her morning meeting.

◁ I walked into school and I'm sure I overheard two girls whisper something about my 'fat thighs'. I have been trying so hard to look after my body in a healthy way and this really made me feel mad (and really upset too).

◁ Susan made a TikTok video and I know her comment about losers was directed at me.

◁ I got my history test back and even though I studied really hard, I only got 57%. This really, really upset me.

◁ The cherry on top after a day like today was when Dad was late to pick me up. I got into the car, feeling upset about the hectic day I had had and he started going off at me about my sulky attitude. I just can't any more! I arrived home, stomped through the lounge and into my bedroom. I heard Mom say, 'What's her problem?' She really doesn't get it and doesn't even try to understand me. I can't control what's happening inside and I feel like a bubbling volcano. I slammed the door and burst into tears on my bed. It's official. I am having a 'meltdown'.

HOLDING THE SPACE FOR VERY HUMAN STATES

Anger, sadness, tantrums, defiance – all the 'behaviours' you would rather not see (which are so developmentally appropriate #*JustSaying*) – are simply a symptom of a human being in a state of dysregulation. Human beings in a state of dysregulation need the presence of other human beings who can remain regulated.

Being nearby without reacting and being able to contain our child's emotions in a bigger bucket while their buckets overflow into ours means that we are 'holding that space' for them.

We need to allow their buckets to spill over into ours, catch their overfill and hold this space safely for them.

We as adults have more emotional and cognitive ability to process big emotions. When we manage to hold that space without becoming dysregulated ourselves, that's when we are really helping our children's brains do some serious growth!

This is exactly why we need to work on self-care and regulation as a priority at *all* times. Drilling holes in our buckets to empty ourselves of our emotional overwhelm and stress ensures that we have the capacity to sit near our children in regulated states.

With teens you may be holding the space from outside their bedroom door and that's okay. What's important for our children and our relationship with them is that they know that when the storm is over there was an adult who stood alongside them while it raged. There was an adult who didn't run away, who didn't push them aside and didn't feel scared of the storm within them. When our children feel that we abandon them when they're in their big emotional spaces, to them, that's rejection. When children feel rejected, the message they take on board is that parts of them are unlovable and are 'too much' to deal with. This then reflects on their sense of self and their resilience.

DRILLING THE HOLES

What do you need to do to reduce your overwhelm and stress? Maybe it's a walk on a nature trail, a gym workout, a cup of tea with your beloved pet or an 'alone-time' bubble bath.

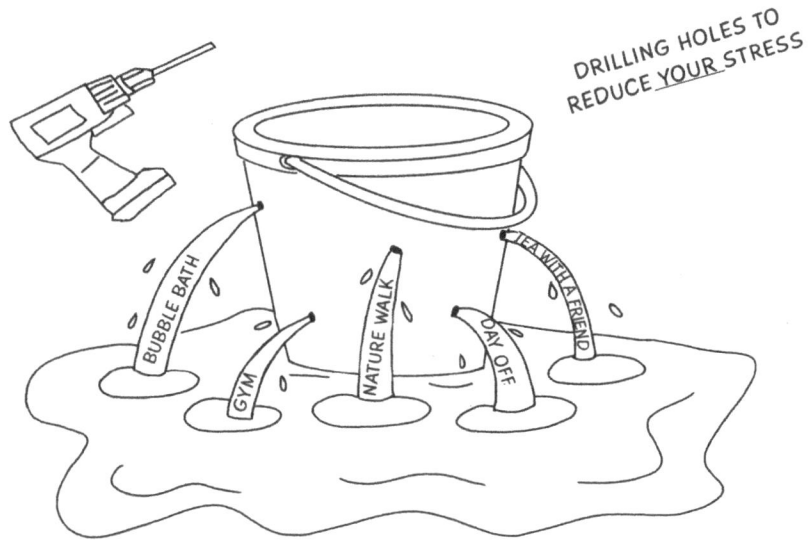

Whatever drilling holes in your bucket means for you, do more of that. Prioritise it daily. It's not possible to hold that space for others if you don't practise self-care! And that's a required CC Moment right there!

MY BUCKET-DRILLING PLANS:

_____

_____

_____

_____

_____

_____

_____

_____

_____

MELTDOWNS ACROSS ALL AGES

Meltdowns are not just a toddler issue. Human beings of all ages have meltdowns – they may look slightly different at our different age stages, but we all have them. These very out-of-control experiences happen when we are feeling dysregulated.

In any situation where our brain is triggered to feel less than safe to any degree, it activates a survival state. In this state our 'thinking' upper brain disconnects from the lower brain regions so that it can take over and keep us alive.

You may know that there is no imminent danger to your toddler when the cereal bowl isn't available. *You* may be fully aware that it is not a life-or-death situation when your teen's 'crush' doesn't text back immediately. But *their* brain's stress response has been triggered and releases the stress hormones cortisol, adrenaline and noradrenaline into their systems. This cascade of survival hormones results in psychological responses like shallow breathing, rapid heart rate, shakiness, a rush of strength and feelings of physical and emotional vulnerability.

These responses could present as anger, a fountain of tears, irrational verbal outpourings or all of the above, but they are actually the sympathetic nervous system that's been triggered into a state of fight and flight. Your child and/or teen at this point has no – and I mean zero, zilch, nada – control over their emotional and psychological responses to their environment (including you if you are in it).

You may be yelling things like 'Stop it!', 'Don't be ridiculous', 'It's not that bad!' or numerous profanities, but at that exact moment they cannot access their rational brains. In fact, any reactive, defensive and accusatory responses from you are likely exacerbating the dysregulation and alarm state in their bodies. To calm their brains what they need the most is that big calm bucket that is a regulated YOU.

 REMINDER: A calm brain calms an uncalm brain. (There's that really important sentence again!)

This is not a likely possibility when you are stressed out and triggered by your child's big emotions, and is far more likely to happen when you are not doing that 'couch work', not working on destressing and not doing something every day to drill those darn bucket holes. Your child needs a big holey bucket so be exactly that for them!

> We often forget that our kids are human too and they are allowed to have hard days, sad days, irritable days and any other kind of day. Think about how you feel on an 'off' day and what you need at those times. Honour your children enough to give them the compassion that you need on those kinds of days.

THE TRIVIAL IS ACTUALLY NOT SO TRIVIAL AT ALL

Often the things that really distress our children may seem so 'pathetic' or 'inconsequential' to us. Like a young child not being able to have the blue shirt because it's in the washing machine. Or a teen having to miss a party because there's no logistical way to get them there. Our swirling thoughts of 'For goodness sake!', 'It's not the end of the world' or 'It's just one party' are how *we* try to reason through the blue shirt and the missed-party debacles from an adult perspective. But the brain and all its beautifully complex functions develop from the bottom up so primitive survival instincts develop first, then the emotional parts and only then the thinking parts.

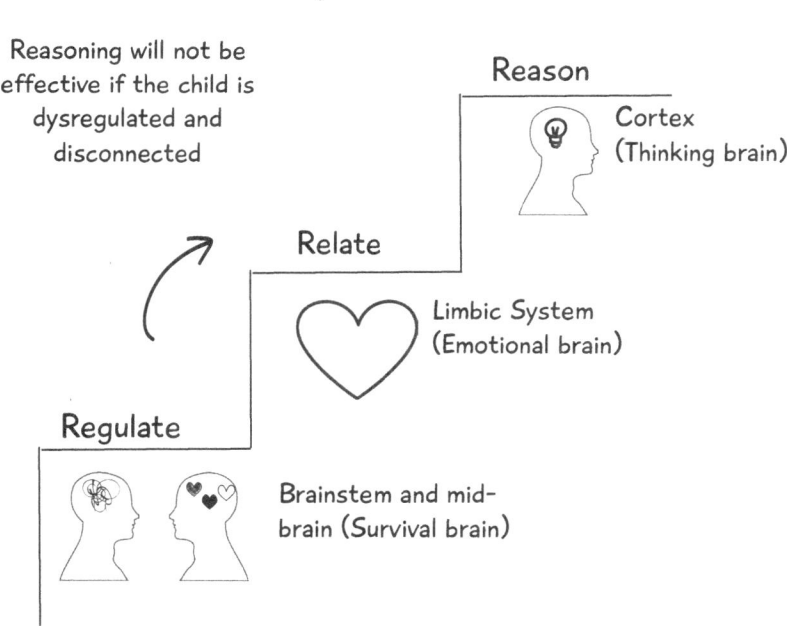

Bruce Perry's 3Rs

Bruce Perry, the well-known American psychiatrist, talks about the three Rs: Regulate, Relate and Reason. When we are dealing with big emotional meltdowns (of any human being of any age), the three Rs create a base to work from to help your child (or anyone in that state) manage their massive emotional space.

The first R is to regulate. When the primitive survival brain parts are activated, we can't access words. They are meaningless. When a child or teen or anyone is in this state, say nothing. Go down to their level and sit in their space. But that means you have to be regulated within yourself. If you feel like you're about to lose your cool, rather turn around, take a deep breath and remember 'My child is having a hard time not giving me a hard time'. Sometimes this helps us to change our perspective. Then ask yourself the question, 'What is the one thing that my child needs right now?' In most cases it really is just US, in a calm and connected space of being. Whatever you have to do to get into this space, do it!

The second R is to relate. This is where we may empathise using vocabulary to describe what we think our child may be feeling and continue to stay in their space without trying to fix the problem or sweep away the big emotions. Obviously, if your teen has kicked you out of the room, hang around and be nearby. They know and feel if you are hanging around or 'walking away'.

As tempting as it might be to storm off, it is in these moments of their greatest vulnerability that they need you the most. Your presence speaks volumes to them about their worth and value in the world and to you. When we walk away, often our children feel further rejection and embrace the message that they aren't good enough. This doesn't help them to learn how to regulate.

Only *then* do we get to the third and final step – reason. This is seldom at the 'heated' time because when the brain is not calm it cannot access the reasoning parts anyway. Your attempts to rationalise, explain or even teach when the brain is still in survival or emotional states are not only futile but might even cause your child to become more frustrated. The reasoning may only come later that night or even the next day when we can speak to our child's or teen's rational brain. That is when we can discuss what happened, why they felt the way they did and talk about if there may be better ways that they could try to respond to the situation the next time.

REMINDER: A child will not listen until they feel heard and understood. Too often as adults we talk too much and we think our role is to give advice. It's not. We need to learn to be quiet and listen because only then can children trust us enough to listen back and allow us to guide them.

If you try to go straight for the logic, you're going to miss the connection opportunity entirely and it's very likely that your child is only going to end up feeling frustrated and angry because they feel like you don't 'get it'.

THE IMPORTANCE OF WORDS

So many adults lack the ability to express how they are feeling and they tend to be angry, depressed, avoidant or highly anxious as a result. Whenever any of us are in states of big, overwhelming emotions we are like bubbling volcanoes. When we have the words to describe how we are feeling we can prevent these volcanoes from erupting. It is vital to teach our children from the youngest age about all the different emotions and give them the words to describe how they are feeling. There are a number of ways to do this, but talking about *your* emotions, their emotions and the emotions of people all around you is a good way to begin.

When our kids know that there is a word to describe what they are feeling, they'll also be able to see that all emotional states are normal because other people feel them too. When we give our kids and teens the words to express themselves, there's a much greater chance that they will feel understood and believe that you 'get it'.

This is the interpretation happening on the inside: When I understand how I'm feeling I can put things into place to help me get through the wave of emotion. It's a useful analogy to use the visual of a wave to describe to your kids and teens how emotions aren't permanent states. They come and they go and they can feel pretty overwhelming when they're at their peak, but they don't stay like that. All waves reach the shore and fizzle to foam. Knowing that the overwhelm will pass helps all of us believe that we can get through even the most disempowering states.

EMOTIONS ARE LIKE
WAVES –
THEY COME AND GO.

From a neurological perspective, when we can even just name *what* we are feeling, we can shift the part of our brain that we are using to access the more rational prefrontal-cortex zone. In my home and at my practice, I use a set of emotion-faced cards to help the kids and teens I work with, as well as my own children, understand and name their emotions. (Refer to the resource section at the end of the book for more details.)

My kids love the cards so much that they often ask me for them. When they're in a big state of overwhelm, they grab the pack that stays in an easily accessible kitchen drawer and go through the cards one by one to pick out all the emotions they are feeling. We put these cards to one side and then go through them one at a time and talk about the emotions. This is empowering for them and it's also very connecting as my children know that I then completely understand the space that they are in. That's exactly what we as human beings of *all* ages need – to feel validated, valued, heard and understood.

THE number-one thing that makes a child feel like an 'okay' human being is knowing that in their homes all emotions are normal. They need the message that 'All of me, not only the good, friendly, sweet parts of me, *all parts* of me are lovable'.

THIS is what unconditional love means. It's so much easier to talk about than practise, but the message our children take away from us remains critical: 'Bring it to me. This home is a safe space where you can let it all out.' When we don't create that, we see disconnection, depression and anxiety.

Talk about emotions with your children as often as you talk about putting the clothes in the laundry basket. Talk about them at the dinner table, in the car, when discussing the books that you read and in the movies you watch together. When we talk too much about any topic people tend to 'check out' of the conversation mentally. Although we don't want to tire our kids out with these kinds of conversations, we do want the topic of emotions to be woven into our daily lives and the everyday talks we have with our children. This has been invaluable in my home and has enabled my children to feel safe coming to me about any overwhelming aspect of their lives.

LET'S TALK ABOUT ONIONS

Anger is a fascinating emotion and what I call the 'onion' emotion. It's the only human emotion that isn't single-layered. Anger is never just anger; at its core it is always disempowerment. The layers between disempowerment and the volcanic eruption that presents as anger are filled with other emotions such as pain, fear, grief, sadness and guilt.

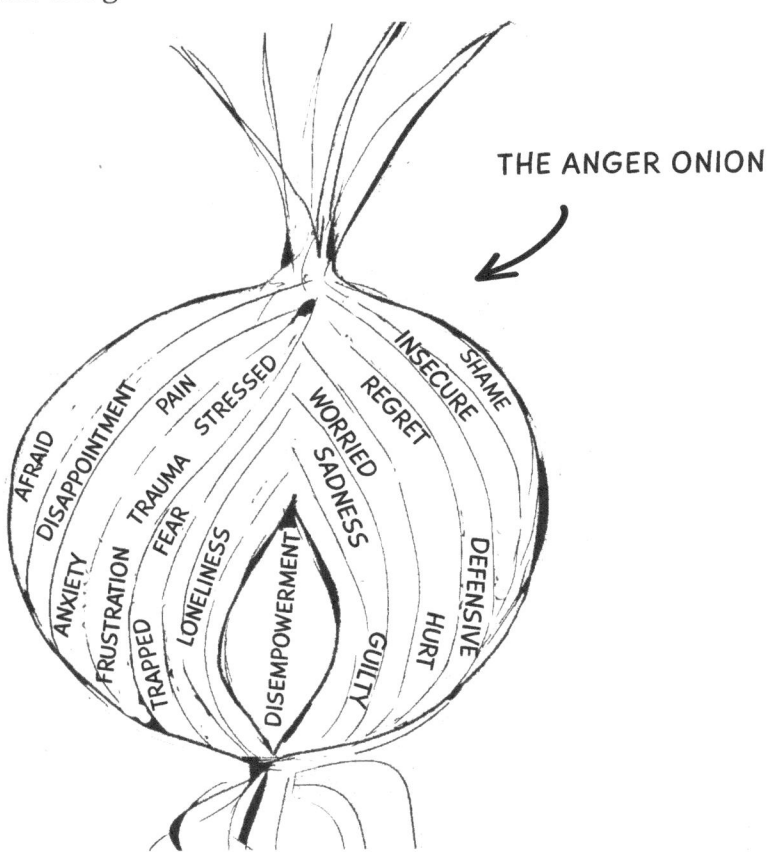

THE ANGER ONION

When we react to our children's anger not only do we disconnect, but we also miss the real message that their behaviour is trying to communicate. Often an angry child is simply a child in emotional pain and distress. When we can reframe anger as pain that is trying to find a voice, it enables us to respond to it with more compassion and meet the need behind the rage. Anger is a defence against vulnerability. It enables us to keep 'the other' out in an attempt to keep our hurt from deepening by letting anyone get too close. This applies to human beings of *all* ages, not just our kids and teens.

BEING THE PUNCHBAG

When our children are angry, as parents we often end up becoming their punchbags. No one likes being the emotional punchbag and it's not a quality we desire to add to our 'parenting honour badge'. However, our sad and wounded children punch where they know they will find a soft landing space and often we *are* it. They punch where it feels safe and they punch when they are feeling desperately unsafe.

Your first response may well be: 'Well, if they need help then why the heck are they pushing me away?' I hear this so often and the truth is that that's what any of us do when we are in excruciating pain. We tortoise (climb into our shells and hide away from the world for a while) or we lash out (anger being a common response to the vulnerability we feel when we are in pain). Our actions merely reflect the extent of our vulnerability and hurt.

Our natural response to anger is to strike back, get ourselves worked up, send our kids away, storm off ourselves, or punish their anger because often what they say and do feel hurtful to us. This is when we need to ask ourselves what our very hurting child needs right in that moment and what they are trying to tell us.

 NOTE: I said ask OURSELVES not them because THEY likely won't be able to tell you, especially not in their very emotional and angry state. When we can hold that space, let what doesn't really matter go, not take the bait and keep going back, time and time again, with arms loaded full of unconditional love, eventually the anger softens, pain erupts, tears flow ... and only then can connection happen. Only then can the healing process begin. This is not easy or tear-free for us as parents and requires so much patience and many, many, many moments of self-compassion.

A few years ago, I was an emotional punchbag for an entire year. It was utterly painful and raw, but in retrospect the very sore emotions that I was left feeling as a result of being that punchbag, were just a reflection of all that could not be expressed, but was actually going on inside my child. There were plenty of days I went to bed feeling emotionally black and blue, bruised from head to toe, and plenty of nights my pillow was damp with the tears of a very heavy-hearted mom. I *knew* there were deep and complex layers underlying the eye-rolls, the defiance, the backchat, the verbal pushbacks and the uncharacteristic actions of a typically very kind-souled child.

Many days I bit my tongue and did plenty of deep breathing. Some days I broke down and sobbed and others I pushed back in desperation. But deep down my mom-heart knew that there was so much more going on so I kept stepping back into the ring with wide open arms. I kept absorbing the emotional punches. I kept believing that the day would come when I would understand why the punches were being thrown and when we would be able to move beyond the fighting ring together.

That day did come. It came shortly after yet another eye-roll and an abrupt reaction when I tapped my child on the shoulder and, like I had so many times before, said, 'Hey, love. I know something else is going on here ... I am here to help ...'

This little person spun around and clung to me like a koala bear for 40 minutes. Forty MINUTES of sobbing. Forty minutes of holding. Forty minutes of a heartbreaking story of exclusion and aloneness – of grief. I held and held as the tears silently cascaded down my cheeks too.

It was a year of pain that was so excruciating for both of us that words couldn't even be expressed so these words were held within, until they found their escape through what my child and I together termed 'Sangriness'.*

*Sangriness: /sangri/adjective INFORMAL
Bad-tempered or irritable as a result of sadness.

From the day the 'Sanger' found the purity of expression in sadness and didn't need to hide behind a pillar of anger, healing started and new life sprung.

I often reflect on my year as that punchbag. If I had reacted, pushed away, or punished, all I would have done was cause even greater pain in my child. I would have reinforced the seed that had begun growing within my child that they were not good enough, not valuable enough, not worthy of being loved. Those reactions would have resulted in a deep depression.

Those 40 minutes of heartbreaking truth were the moments of deepest connection and were the start of the healing process for both of us. When my child finally realised that I understood the months and months of Sanger and that I was determined to help make the changes that were needed in the environment for them to find happiness again, suddenly we were a team working together on a problem. That made ALL the difference.

My bruises have healed and my child is thriving. We've changed how we talk about anger in my home. When I notice that one of my children is angry, I don't question the anger. I say, 'Hey, love, I can see you're feeling sangry and I'm here if you want to talk about it. If you don't want to that's okay, but I am here.' They get that I 'get' the complexity and pain.

There are going to be so many times when you'll be called on to be that safe landing space. Don't react. Just absorb and keep standing there, with arms open wide.

DEFIANCE

Defiance is one of the many facets of reactive behaviour. A lot of parents want answers and step-by-step instructions on what to do to put an end to this. Defiance often leads to you placing yourself on one side of the fence with your child on the other side. This separation between you often means that the perception is a 'right' side and a 'wrong' side. We tend to place our kids as always being on the 'wrong' side of that fence. But that fence between you means connection can't happen, and in a state of isolation without connection, resilience is nothing more than a fairy-tale idea.

I don't like the word 'defiance'. It's a word that immediately conjures up images of a revoltingly behaved, attitude-filled, young human being. Kids and teens don't intentionally behave badly. Perhaps your first reaction to this is to throw your arms up and yell out loud that I clearly have no idea about the atrocity of the behaviour and the obvious degree of defiance happening in your home.

 Here's what you need to remember: The more 'revolting' the behaviour, the more desperate the message behind it is and the more urgent it becomes for us to meet the need. (For extra info and a reminder, refer back to the section on teen brain development in Attribute 7.)

If your child's 'defiant' behaviour seems to be 'intentional', there's an emotional need that they do not feel is being met. When we really get to the bottom of it and meet the need, the behaviour changes. We can see this in human beings of all ages. When any of us have 'full emotional buckets' the way we respond to our world and treat others is completely different to when our buckets are empty. If you are a parent of a tween or teen, this next sentence may be hard to digest, but may also bring some comfort. 'Defiance' is an important part of our older children finding their independence from us. It's (here we go!) developmentally appropriate and actually even emotionally healthy.

 NOTE: I didn't say it wasn't extremely frustrating at times.

When your child is defiant and their behaviour is pushing you away, that's exactly when you need to dig deep and show up. Keep showing up. Be there and let it go. Respond to the emotional vulnerability with reflection and empathy instead of reacting to the behaviour. You're *not* reinforcing negative behaviour if you respond compassionately; you are creating a safe space for a dysregulated body and brain and a foundation for a much stronger relationship between you and your child. These are the moments when resilience is being developed and your child or teen is reminded that you love them unconditionally – *no matter what!*

'LOVE ME WHEN I LEAST DESERVE IT. BECAUSE THAT'S WHEN I MOST NEED IT.'
Swedish proverb

I made this quote into a fridge magnet that has become my daily reminder. These words are some of the ones I need to bring to mind most often in my parenting – especially when 'defiant-like' behaviours that may send me into a spin are going down in my home. The simple truth of these words is so powerful.

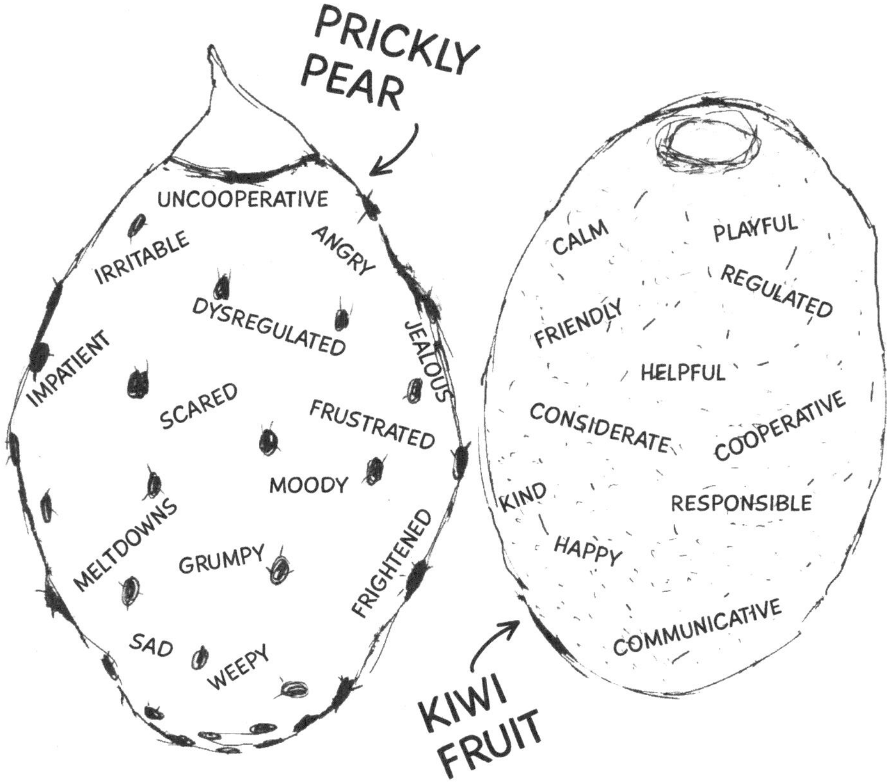

PRICKLY PEAR

UNCOOPERATIVE

IRRITABLE

ANGRY

IMPATIENT

DYSREGULATED

JEALOUS

SCARED

FRUSTRATED

MOODY

MELTDOWNS

GRUMPY

FRIGHTENED

SAD

WEEPY

CALM

PLAYFUL

REGULATED

FRIENDLY

HELPFUL

CONSIDERATE

COOPERATIVE

KIND

RESPONSIBLE

HAPPY

COMMUNICATIVE

KIWI FRUIT

PRICKLY PEARS AND KIWI FRUIT

In our house we talk about whether we'd describe ourselves as a prickly pear or a kiwi fruit, depending on how we're feeling. Bear with me on the fruit analogy! If you're irritable or easily upset you're feeling prickly like a prickly pear. If you're happy and zesty, life feels great like a scrumptious kiwi fruit! It's a human phenomenon – different actions and emotional spaces result in the production of different fruit.

 In those difficult moments, when my kids are having a rough

day and being a little 'prickly' and after many deep breaths on my part, I'll ask my son if he wants a hug to help him feel 'more like a kiwi?' Taking his primary love language of physical touch into consideration, I am making that connection with him. I'll ask my daughter if I can spend a few moments of quiet alone time with her; her primary love language is quality time. Often, depending on the degree of 'prickle', no words are needed in any of these interactions – just the hug or the quiet time. (The concept of love languages is discussed in more detail in Attribute 12.)

With so much going on in our noisy and frantic world, prickly pears are in abundance in many of our kids and teens. Find small 'check-in' moments. Ask the quiet question and infuse the power phrase in those side-by-side times: 'Are you doing okay? I am here.'

When I notice that my kids are going through a prickly pear stage, I make extra effort to do those 'check-ins'. I play a quick game (which creates a powerfully connecting space), find those quiet moments 'after lights out' or before sunrise when the rest of the world is still in darkness.

Anywhere you can find a quiet bubble with them, check in by connecting in the way that makes your child feel the most loved (important note: a check-in doesn't need to mean talking through things or asking questions). Your child may not always respond in the way you would like them to, and they may not be able to tell you why they are feeling 'prickly', but that's not what matters. What matters is that you *noticed* and that they know their prickles won't keep you away.

When prickly pears feel loved and heard most often they transform into kiwis pretty quickly. This is particularly true in our tweens and teens whose prickles can seem even more offensive, relentless and harder to deal with at times than those of our younger children. Just be still, listen, stay quiet and keep loving them. All prickly pears are really just kiwis in hiding!

My son wrote me this 'kiwi' note at a restaurant after a particularly prickly pear incident. You can tell from the note that his love language is physical touch and his nervous system is very much regulated through hugs.

~ Attribute 10 ~

PARENTS OF RESILIENT CHILDREN ... DON'T TRY TO 'FIX' THEM

(The last attribute was a whole lot to digest. I am going to give you a breather on this one. It's a great deal shorter but no less important.)

Parents often bring their kids and teens to me with the underlying message that their child needs to be 'fixed'. Your child does not need fixing. They are not broken pieces of equipment.

It's our human nature to want to fix, yet as human beings it is our primary need to feel understood. We always, always, need to seek to understand one another before we try to fix. We need to be comfortable enough to sit in the mud alongside our children instead of trying to sort the problem out, fix things and move on.

When your child is presenting with any kind of difficulty, LISTEN to what they are really trying to communicate without jumping in with an opinion. When they feel that the space is safe and that you really are just 'there' without judgement or advice, they will open up and tell you more. When our protective inner parenting tiger (the one that springs to life as soon as your child enters the world) leaps into the conversation in defensive mode with phrases such as 'I can't believe they did that to you!' or 'You should have reported them to the teacher straight away', it is likely that your child will clam up and you'll no longer feel like that safe, calm space for them to offload their distress.

THE POWER OF QUIET

There are plenty of times that my children tell me about an event that they have perceived as hurtful or unfair – in the classroom, on the playground, on the sports field, in the back yard. It's SO tempting to rush in and offer solutions and question them more. Bad idea! When this happens, *pause* and remember that at the most challenging times in our lives, in those painful moments of the journey, what matters most is knowing that there is someone alongside us who can sit with us through the dark times. That is what our children and teens need so that they can learn to find their own way through the dark patches in life.

There's power in silence. A LOT of power. It's in silence that those CC moments happen, those 'pause-and-think' (and change) moments. This is true for us *and* our kids.

One of the most important things we want our kids and teens to feel is understood. As human beings, when we feel understood we find the strength to do the hard things. And when we do the hard things, we realise we can withstand them. We realise we can walk through fire and survive and we realise we are resilient.

LEAVE YOUR STORY RIGHT THERE

My son likes being at home. He likes his house, his space, his bed (even his pillow matters to him) and he really likes lots of hugs from his family. The thought of being away from any of these comforts sends him spiralling quickly into a pit of despair. When he was nine years old, a school notice arrived in his bag about a one-night class sleepover. It promised heaps of fun – mud, farm animals, zip-lining into dams (all things that he loves) but he hid that notice from me for as long as he could, adamant that he would not be going.

I tried everything to get him to change his mind. I talked about the fun he would have, I empathised and reminded him of all he would be missing out on, but NOTHING was budging him. I had exhausted my 'psychologist toolbox' and my 'mom encouragement' tactics and had all but given up completely. Two days before the form was due to be returned, feeling completely defeated, I turned to him and said, 'I remember when I was nine years old and I had to go on a school camp. I remember telling my mom that I would *not* go and being so upset that this was even happening to me. I loved my home, my parents and my own things so much that I didn't even want to be one night without them. The thought of it made me feel so upset and I started missing everything even before I had left for camp.'

I left that story right there in the middle of the supermarket parking lot and I kept quiet. I didn't try to add, 'So, I think you should go' or 'I was fine and I enjoyed it' or anything along those lines. No convincing, no pushing, no bribery or attempts at manipulation. And then I waited ... About half an hour later, my son piped up from the back seat, 'Mom, I think I may try to go to the sleepover. I said *may* ...' But that was all we needed and he went to the camp and had the best fun ever!

What caused the change? What shifted his brain to even

considering that he *may* want to give it a try? It's the same for all of us. When we know that someone we love *really* understands what we are feeling and we know someone has 'gone before us' and come out on the other side, then we have the confidence to do hard things.

Telling your children or teens a story about when you were their age and in a similar situation, *without* trying to fix or direct their decision afterwards, tells them they're normal and they're not alone. Most often, we find all the bravery and courage we need to attempt the 'scary' as soon as we know this.

≋ Attribute 11 ≋

PARENTS OF RESILIENT CHILDREN ... PRIORITISE PLAY AND
HAVE FUN

We connect through play. It's essential for development and
it's essential for healing and growth. Play is how our children
communicate. It is their language, yet we live in a world where due to
rushing, busyness and overloaded schedules, our children and teens
have fewer and fewer opportunities to play. So much of our parenting
can be summed up as barking instructions at our children from the
minute they wake up in the morning until they go to sleep at night.

6:00am: 'Wake up, my love.'
6:15am: 'It's really time to wake up, my love.'
6:30am: 'I'm going to end up leaving without you!'
6:45am: 'Eat your breakfast. Brush your teeth. Get your bag.'
7:00am: 'I'm leaving with or without you in that car!'
3:00pm: 'Have you got any homework?'
3:15pm: 'Please get changed out of your school clothes and do your homework.'
4:00pm: 'Have you packed your bag for tomorrow?'
5:00pm: 'Shower time!'
6:00pm: 'Please set the table.'
6:30pm: 'Dinner time!'
7:00pm: 'Brush your teeth, please. Read a book. Why are your clothes on the floor AGAIN!?'
8:00pm: 'Bedtime. I'm switching off the light. Sweet dreams.'

A day's worth of 'doing' and no time for 'being', for connecting, for fun. This is too often the case and there's no possible room for our kids to thrive, let alone have time to breathe.

Play is everything in a child's world. We should be getting out of our world and climbing into theirs and playing alongside them. Play is great for processing emotions, nervous-system regulation, communication, strengthening relationships, ensuring that our children feel loved and valued, and for so many more researched benefits below.

✔ Play stimulates early brain development.
✔ Play improves intelligence.
✔ Creative thinking is sparked during play.
✔ Vocabulary, communication and language are improved.

✔ Impulse control and emotional regulation are promoted.

✔ Social competence and empathy are grown.

✔ Play improves physical and mental health.

✔ Problem-solving skills develop.

✔ Peer and family relationships are strengthened.

Let your kids play – not planned, structured, colour-by-number-type play. Let them be who they are naturally developing to be within the awesomeness of play. If you're feeling down and have no inspiration, here is a sure-fire way to turn things around: put on 'Gangnam Style' by South Korean rapper Psy and see what happens. You'll probably all be dancing around together even if it becomes part of getting dressed and ready for school. Try it!!!

THE POWER OF PLAY

I was *that* parent during lockdown. The one who didn't do the 'pandemic schooling'. I was working online trying to respond to the need in overwhelming numbers of people struggling with the things that would be expected during those unprecedented times – anxiety, depression, fear, overwhelm. The last thing I had the physical or emotional capacity for at the end of an online day was arguing with a child who struggled with schooling anyway.

Secondly, and more importantly, I knew that the most important aspect necessary for healing through any trauma is connection and hitting heads about insisting that my at-the-time six-year-old child needed to sit down and painstakingly complete what he felt were tedious school tasks was only going to result in a disconnection within our relationship.

The world out there was such an unstable, uncertain and trauma-filled place and I wanted to preserve the safety of our relationship above all else. So, after about day three, I called it quits. I let my kids (my daughter was four at the time) redesign the garden with forts, climb every tree in the garden, create every masterpiece they could dream up with the art supplies we had. They built, invented, engineered, explored and experimented the way children naturally do when we as adults don't contaminate the process.

By the end of the four months, a few days before we were due to head back to school in late June, my distorted and unhelpful mom-guilt kicked in and I suddenly wondered whether my little guy was going to be the only one who was far behind in 'academics'.

I called him to the table and pulled out his writing book that he had last written in at the start of March before the lockdown period. I asked him to write a sentence. The result was astounding and was solid proof of the power of play. Without any 'practice', his writing had decreased significantly in size, his letter formation had improved and he was able to string a reasonable written sentence together.

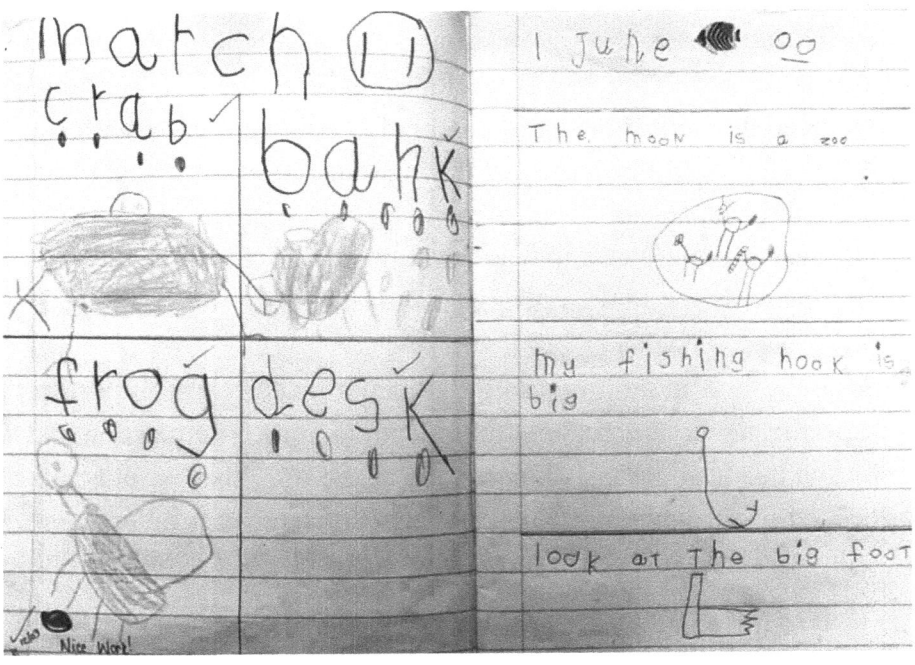

Never underestimate the power of play to heal, to connect and to support all aspects of development. It's like a magic glitter that benefits and brightens everything it touches.

PLAY IS THE SPRINGBOARD OF RELATIONSHIPS

I'm sure that before you got married (and if you aren't married, while you were dating or before you made a long-term commitment to each other), you and your partner laughed. A lot. You had fun and did all kinds of things together. I'm sure there were few formalities involved unless you're in an arranged marriage perhaps.

Connection and relationships are built on fun. THAT's how you build meaningful bonds.

There is often a skewed perception of what a parent-child relationship should look like. In the busyness of our days, there's very little time for playing and connection. But without laughter and fun, it's impossible to build healthy relationships.

Play is the primary language of a child. Actually, it's the primary language of all of us. If your children aren't listening, it may be because you aren't speaking in their mother tongue. It's not up to our children to connect to our world and understand our (grown-up) language. We need to speak *their* language, which turns out to be a healthy one for us all to remember.

I know we are all busy moms and dads who constantly have to be in 20 places at the same time and I realise that not everything can be done and said playfully. But when it can be done playfully, do it. Too often we are too serious.

The best memories aren't made when we're yelling daily humdrum orders. The business of bonding is fun and, along with those bubble moments, that's where so many of the interactions that create the foundation of resilience are formed.

THE GROUND-LEVEL EXAMPLES

I'm sure many of you will relate to the following scenario when it comes to the routine of daily life.

Laundry never seems to find its way into the laundry basket at our house. It's just too attached to the floor or the lid of the basket and never seems to find its way *inside*. And no amount of begging, pleading, yelling or demonstrating can get those clothes in that container. Most nights I walk past the bathroom and notice that, once again, there is laundry on the floor. Right next to the lid. All that is needed is for someone to lift the lid ever so slightly and gently push those dirty clothes inside. No energy required!

And every night (and I mean *every* night) that I see the items on the floor, an exasperated irritation arises. Sometimes a part of me wants to yell, and sometimes I am so tired that I just sweep the items up and plonk them where they're meant to go. Here's the fun part that changes the entire evening. Very often, once I have done my deep, regulated breathing, in a silly, pretend-to-be-shocked voice I say something like, 'Oh my goodness! We've got a major problem. There are escapees! There are escapees in the bathroom! HELP! Let's get these things into the laundry basket quickly!'

It's at this point that my kids laugh and rush to help me put their dirty laundry in the basket. If I had lost it with them, I would have disconnected from them. I would have become dysregulated, their nervous systems would have gone into a state of stress and none of us would have felt good. This 'snappy' reaction does not build resilience.

Does this 'playful parenting' mean that the next day the laundry is going to be in the laundry basket? Probably not, but I've turned a household chore into something more connected and likely enjoyable. Like singing opera to my children while brushing their teeth when they were little. Or being 'a bird looking for grass in a hippo's teeth' or 'risking my feathered life looking for scraps of smelly rotten meat in a crocodile's teeth'. When it comes to adding play into your parenting, think creatively.

Play is the most empowering aspect for a child and teen in a chaotic world. It is what we should be pursuing as much and as often as possible. Wherever it can be done playfully, do it playfully.

 Creative thinking requires a parent who has had adequate sleep and isn't running on fumes. For most parents when I mention the words 'adequate sleep' they laugh or roll their eyes, but we need to do everything possible to stop putting sleep at the end of our priority list.

You cannot parent playfully in a regulated state if you are exhausted. When it's possible to make sleep a priority instead of bingeing a Netflix series, sleep! Make sleep a priority because it's really hard to have a sense of humour when you don't.

 Side note: Research and studies have shown that a lack of play in childhood is a contributing factor to depression, chronic stress-related illness and criminal behaviour in adulthood. THAT is the power of play.

Playing doesn't come naturally to everyone and that's okay! If you feel weird and uncomfortable trying to get down on your child's level, here are a few ideas that might alleviate that awkwardness of not knowing 'how' to play with them.

Babies (0–2 years):
Keep it simple. Their favourite toy is you. Babble along, talk back to their coos, reflect their facial expressions. Clap and smile in response to any attempt at engagement from their side. This is their play world.

It's important to watch for signs of overstimulation though as this means it's time for calm, quiet connection, not loud and exciting parent feedback! Babies who are overstimulated may:

◁ Cover their eyes or face
◁ Cry excessively
◁ Grimace
◁ Turn their head away
◁ Wave and kick their legs in an agitated way
◁ Appear glassy-eyed and limp
◁ Act fussy and irritable
◁ Clench their fists.

These are all indications that you need to quiet and slow things down – rock them, read to them in a calm voice and sit with them in a dimly lit room.

Pre-schoolers (3–6 years):
Kids of this age love using their imagination. Put on your 'pretend hat', dress up, jump the horses, be the kid when they want to play 'teacher-teacher', get out the playdough, build with blocks, wrestle on the couch. Most importantly, your child needs to control the play. The hard part is to let yourself be controlled, but this is the empowering part for your child and where they feel like their world actually matters to you.

Primary-school children (6–12 years):
This is when you can start playing more rule-based games as these fascinate children aged six and older. Within reason, let them choose when and what they want to play. Whether it's tag, garden cricket, board games, Lego, cycling, tennis, baking — follow their interests and get into their world. Unstructured play where they can just 'be' is also important at this age.

Teens (13–18 years):
Spend side-by-side time with teens, walking, cooking, watching movies, doing any sport they enjoy. Ask them about their favourite music and Instagram influencer, get googling and get into their worlds. Find out as much as you can about their interests and, without judging, get curious. It does transformative things for relationships of all ages when one party feels like the other is really making an effort to engage and understand. You may not like the tunes or the hairstyles of the people your teens idolise, but if it's not hurting anyone, keep your opinion to yourself and show interest. Keep the family meals going and include a games evening of their choice. Just be there and listen.

A LITTLE WORD WITH A BIG IMPACT

We often use a certain word with our children. A very little word that is so powerful in the message it sends them to them.

Later.

How often do our children ask us to do something and our response is 'Later'?

When my daughter was about three or four years old, we travelled to Mozambique and had been driving all day. It had been a 2am start, but I hadn't slept the night before with all the packing, attending to last-minute emails and ensuring there was enough sunscreen, mozzie repellent, a stocked first-aid box and all the favourite teddies. Just as parenting and big holiday preparation always go.

When we finally arrived at our destination it was about 4:30pm and my daughter pulled out some blue playdough. I found myself a hammock on the veranda of our rustic beach cottage and was just soaking up the complete nothingness of the late afternoon because, cognitively and physically, I wasn't actually capable of much more. Then I heard a little voice, 'Mom, please come and play. Come and make playdough cakes with me.'

Utterly exhausted, I responded, 'Later, my love.'

She waited a few minutes and then she said again, 'Mom, please come and make playdough cakes with me.'

I again said, 'Later, love.'

After she asked me the third time and I responded with the same reply, she said something that I'll never forget. 'Mom, when will later be?'

At that moment, the realisation slammed me. She was absolutely right. Later, later, later. She was inviting me into her world and I was communicating (through my words and non-verbal actions) that I wasn't interested in getting into it. I was communicating that she wasn't valuable. That her world wasn't important and that what mattered to her didn't matter much at all.

I got up from my hammock, sat alongside her and made blue playdough cakes. I took a few minutes to be with her in the activity that had captured her imagination, and it regulated both of us. You don't have to always stop what you are doing and immediately do something that your child asks of you, but you can spend time engaging even if it is showing an interest while they play alongside you when you are doing some of the unavoidable things that come with being a grown-up.

Don't put off playing with your kids. When you do you are missing the opportunity for connection. One day they won't want to play any more and these opportunities for connection will have been lost.

THE LANGUAGE OF CHILDREN

When your child asks you to play, pay attention. Get down or get 'up' to their level. If they're asking for connection and you don't give it, the end result is very likely going to be all the behaviours you really don't want to see. The five minutes that it takes to connect over a game of UNO, to throw a few cricket balls in the garden, Hot Wheels passage-racing, or horse-jumping across bedroom obstacles are going to be a whole lot less than the amount of time you are likely going to require to help your child regulate after a meltdown. Or the time you will need to repair the relationship after any disconnection resulting from your own dysregulation in these moments. Play – it's powerful and preventative. This realisation is so often a light-bulb/penny-dropping moment for parents that I work with!

PLAY FOR YOU

When did you last engage in fun and laughter? When was the last time *you* played? What does playing mean for you? Perhaps it's a games night with your family or book club with your girlfriends or fishing with the guys. Maybe it's throwing a ball to your dog. Maybe it's picking up a paintbrush. Maybe it's going for a walk. Maybe it's dancing around the kitchen. Maybe it's just laughing out loud. So often I find myself being silly and doing ridiculous things in my 'play mode'. Whatever you need to do for you to play, have fun and connect, do that. Ignite that child within you because that inner child is a part of you for your whole life.

Our kids need to see that as adults we haven't forgotten how to have fun, how to relax and how to connect with one another through laughter. Whatever play means in your adult life is essential for our regulation and mental health. So do more of that. Schedule it in as a priority, not as a 'that-would-be-great-but-I-don't-have-time' activity.

And for anyone in the education profession, in the stress-filled world we are living in, PLAY, not curriculum, is what we should be pursuing at all costs. There is plenty of research showing the benefits of learning through play, including improved social skills and knowledge retention.

> 'YOU CAN DISCOVER MORE
> ABOUT A PERSON IN AN HOUR
> OF PLAY THAN IN A YEAR OF
> CONVERSATION.'
> Plato

⮑ Attribute 12 ⮐

PARENTS OF RESILIENT CHILDREN ... LISTEN MINDFULLY

Understanding the word 'mindfully' can make a powerful difference in how valued our children feel and consequently how resilient they become. When they feel truly heard and that what they have to say matters, children feel worthy of love in this world.

I shudder to think how many times my kids have said to me, 'Mom, did you hear what I said?' or instances when my brain 'clicks' that it's *me* that they are talking to. Or you know that feeling when you register that whatever they are saying has already been uttered a few times previously?

Alarmingly, studies show that 47% of our waking hours we are not actually mindfully present wherever we are. When I first heard that statistic, I remember thinking there was no way that was accurate, but then I tried to track my thoughts for a few days and realised in horror just how true this is. Almost half of the time our brains are not consciously present in the moment. So often our minds are elsewhere so we might be talking to someone but we're thinking about what we're going to say next and therefore not listening. We are jogging through the forest, but thinking about the emails we need to send. We drive to work on a kind of personal autopilot and arrive where we need to be, but haven't been consciously aware of the actual driving process or taken cognisance of the things that we passed along the way. Our minds are most often running with at least 20 tabs open at once!

Another time I become blatantly aware of the validity of this shocking 47% figure is when I'm driving and I suddenly realise my kids are talking to me from the back seat, saying the same sentence – FOR THE THIRD TIME! But my mind has been elsewhere so when they say, 'Mom, I'm talking to you!' it's a heavy parenting realisation of just how easily we become distracted and unavailable to our children, even when we are sitting less than a metre away from them in a car.

I know a lot of you (I'm looking at you, moms!) might think you can multitask because that's a term we have become used to in modern life. The reality is that you can't! From a neurological perspective, it is not possible for the brain to be in two places at once or fully engage in several tasks simultaneously.

When my daughter was about two years old, I was in the kitchen cutting up veggies on the chopping board.

She came to me and said, 'Mom, look at me.'

I said, 'Yes, right, talk to me. I'm listening,' and I carried on cutting and chopping.

She said, 'Mom, look at me.'

I said, 'My love, I'm listening.'

She asked again and admittedly, by this point, we were both becoming a bit frustrated.

Eventually she said to me, 'Mom, look at me with your eyes.'

She knew at the age of two that if I was doing something else, there was no way I could actually hear, digest or connect to what she wanted to tell me.

We need to learn to pay attention.

The greatest gift we can give our children isn't anything that we can buy them. It's the gift of our presence – our mindful presence.

GETTING HONEST ABOUT DEVICES

Devices connect us to everything and everyone outside our home and if your home is anything like mine, Mr Google comes out at least once a day and has taken over from the trusty 1980s' encyclopaedias.

It gives us access to so much information, but it can also be so contaminating. The devices that keep us connected to everyone we are away from can very easily disconnect us from the people living under the same roof as us.

Every time we are with our children, whether it's playing a game, hanging out, chatting or eating a meal, and the phone goes 'ping!' we disconnect. In those moments our attention goes straight to our phone. If you are in the presence of your children and your attention leaves the space, you are giving them the message 'This device is more important than you right now'.

As a society, most of us are addicted to the 'pings', the 'likes' and everything else that makes us feel as if the outside world wants us. But that is not the message I want to be giving my kids when I'm meant to be connecting with them, because if that's what they are feeling, it speaks volumes to them about their worth and value. (MOM-TRUTH: Sometimes I arrive home from work and lock my phone away from MYSELF, because there are always messages, clients, or things going on on social media that prevent me from connecting with my kids.)

'Attention is the most basic form of love,' says John Tarrant, a Western Zen teacher, author and the director of the Pacific Zen Institute. This saying is never truer than when applied to the parent-child relationship. Mindful time means being here, now. I know how hard this is but it is so important that we put everything else aside in those moments and let our children know that this is our time with them. Through our actions and choices in these moments, they are left in no doubt that we choose them.

LOVE LANGUAGES

The term 'love languages' was coined by American author Gary Chapman and refers to ways that human beings receive and express love within relationships. These are different for each one of us and are listed as: words of affirmation, quality time, gifts, acts of service and physical touch. We don't receive love through just any language but rather through our *specified* love language/s. Our children have their own love language and it may be completely different to ours. This is important to understand because we may *think* that we are loving our kids more than life itself, yet they may be feeling completely unloved. We may be missing the mark entirely.

It's a significant bonus to understand what love language/s your child speaks and hears in. Every child in your household will have their own unique combination. Many people will have one predominant language and one or two others that they also 'speak'. The list a few pages on shows that ALL of the ideas have the potential to create meaningful connections between you and your child. When you become aware of what your child's dominant language is, just add a little more of that.

My son's primary love language is physical touch. He loves hugs and calls me back to his bed for at least eight hugs a night. He dissolves in back scratches and will often randomly pass us in the passage or kitchen and shout, 'Family hug!' I know that by just pausing when I walk past him and stop to 'check in' with a hug means so much to him. He is also a gifts and acts-of-service child – those are his unique combination of love languages that he speaks and through which he receives love.

My daughter is predominantly a quality-time girl. If you are a busy, stressed, otherwise-occupied-for-any-reason parent, this is a harder love language to speak. It requires pausing what you are doing more often and making sure that when you are with your child, they know that nothing in that moment is more important than your time with them. When we get this right, the appreciation is so evident.

A while ago we were at the beach as a family and I had some urgent work I needed to wrap up so that I could close my laptop and engage with my family for the rest of the holiday period. I had explained to my daughter that as soon as I was done, we would head to the ocean for a dunk in the waves. She waited patiently. And then some more. I soon realised that what I had planned was going to take longer than I thought, so I closed my laptop, put my angst aside and grabbed her hand in mine. 'Let's go!'

She was delighted. As we dived through and jumped over waves, she looked up at me, took my hand and said, 'Mamma, thank you so much for coming to swim with me.'

A tiny act. An hour of uncontaminated time with a little girl when she felt loved and valued. These things matter.

Here are a few ideas to help you connect with your child with the love languages in mind:

PHYSICAL TOUCH
- ✔ Be near your child.
- ✔ Give them lots of physical affection, touches, back scratches and hugs.
- ✔ Have lots of cuddles over story time.
- ✔ Hold hands and give high-fives.
- ✔ Have frequent family hugs.
- ✔ Sit on big bean-bag chairs together.
- ✔ Play games like Twister.
- ✔ Engage in family activities such as fun pillow fights and wrestling games.

WORDS OF AFFIRMATION
- ✔ Say 'I love you' many times in a day and in as many ways as you can.
- ✔ Leave notes in your child's snack box.
- ✔ Notice unique and special things about them and tell them what you see.
- ✔ Call them by their special nickname/your affectionate name for them.
- ✔ Acknowledge all their efforts and perseverance tasks even when the results don't go according to plan.
- ✔ Leave encouraging notes under their pillow or stuck on the mirror.
- ✔ Praise them in front of other people.
- ✔ Speak highly (and loudly!) of your child to others so that your child can hear you.

QUALITY TIME
- ✔ Spend ten minutes after lights-out listening and chatting to each other.

✔ Set parent-child dates and let them see you diarising these dates.

✔ Take your child with you when you run errands.

✔ When they come to you, set aside what you are doing for a moment and pay full attention.

RECEIVING GIFTS

This is an easier love language to speak, especially for busy parents, but be aware that too easily it becomes the only language a parent uses and can result in a child not feeling loved at all.

✔ Find small things you know your child will appreciate and give these to them.

✔ Make small handmade gifts for them.

✔ Pick up things such as unusual rocks or shells on a hike or beach walk.

✔ Pick them flowers from the garden.

✔ Make their favourite dinner and dessert.

ACTS OF SERVICE

✔ Carry their heavy school bags every now and then.

✔ Make them their favourite drink.

✔ Do homework together.

✔ Offer to help them with one of their tasks or chores.

✔ Tuck them into bed at night.

These small acts *really* matter to your child. Identify your child's primary love language and commit to 'talking' to them in that love language every day.

The concept of love languages is all about finding the most effective way to connect with our children in ways that *they* will feel loved, valued and supported.

LOVE BUCKETS

Have you ever asked your child what makes them feel most connected to you? What fills their love bucket?

With life feeling as crazy-chaotic as it does most days, I am always on a complete mission to maximise connection time with my kids. Honestly, it just does not and cannot happen when we're running around on the hazy Formula One track of the typical 'everyday' fluster.

When we are rushed and stressed, we tend to 'coincidentally connect' (if at all) instead of mindfully and meaningfully, and as great as the incidental is and as magical as it can be, I want more for my kids – I want more in my relationship with them.

We disconnect in that rush and that's when the wheels fall off for everyone – more dysregulation, more challenging behaviour, more sibling rivalry, more tear-your-hair-out-while-trying-to-breathe-very-deeply moments. More of all of those are a given.

I want to make SURE that my kids' love buckets are being filled up daily. (Not that I think they must be full because of what I THINK their needs must be.)

PS Their reality may look very different to our presumptions (*#JustSaying*).

Some time back I sat down with my two kids and we drew 'love buckets'. These are now stuck on the fridge as a daily reminder, not for them – FOR ME. When do my children feel the deepest connection?

When I looked at what they told me to write down and what we chatted about, here's the 'adult interpretation':

✔ Mindful, undistracted, fun time together (Undeniably, deep connection happens in these moments of laughter and vulnerability.)

✓ Being given responsibilities and then recognised for doing these (We're talking beaming-like-a-Cheshire-cat material here.)

✓ Physical affection (By the way, when I clarified what they need during 'pricklier' times, both said no matter how much they pushed and performed, they still wanted hugs and me to be near. Exactly what we as adults know from a neurological perspective actually regulates a dysregulated brain.) From the mouths of babes! (#ISayNoMore)

✓ Quiet, one-on-one, deep conversations

✓ Uncontaminated TIME (Yip! Kids really do spell LOVE, T-I-M-E.)

✓ Acknowledgement of who they are and what they do

✓ Family time

✓ When we're all being kind (Because we all know how jolly full of sunshine kindness makes us feel!)

✓ Oh, and of course top of the Animal Empath's list is always 'Being with animals'.

All the beautiful love languages in one bucket spelled out so clearly from the mouths and hearts of my two amazing kids.

Ask your kids what fills their love bucket. And in this ever-chaotic and non-stop world of rush and catch-up, make sure you fill that bucket every day. The positive 'spillage' will have a profound impact on every relationship within your home, and most importantly, on your child's relationship with themselves.

A NOTE ON YOUR CHILD'S SCREEN TIME

There's something that many parents sometimes want to avoid talking about (perhaps it's the elephant calf in many rooms), but it plays a significant role in the quality of connection with our children, which makes it an aspect that I have to mention – however briefly.

I am not going to tell you how much screen time your child should or shouldn't be watching. There are enough books, podcasts, TED talks, research studies and articles to provide you with hundreds of varying opinions. What I *am* going to do is give you some thoughts to consider that are based on experiences from my therapeutic work, the studies that I have read and from my experience as a mom.

As a parent, I understand that sometimes it feels like the only breather you get is when your kids are glued to a screen. Depending on your child's age, there's nothing wrong with a short amount of screen time watching age-appropriate content. If your child is under two years old, however, experts recommend ZERO screen time. I worked with the parents of an 18-month-old who had his own cellphone and iPad and let's just say that the impact on all aspects of his development were utterly detrimental and avoidable.

Being on a screen and gaming is fun for kids, but it's also very addictive. It's an easy world for our kids to get drawn into and it's a hard one for them to extricate themselves from.

What I really want to home in on here is the relationship between screen time and levels of resilience in a child. We know that the foundation of resilience is connection. By this I mean face-to-face human connection – not online screen connection. Our nervous system regulates when we feel safe and connected to another human being – in their actual presence.

Social anxiety across all age groups is at an all-time high, given that during the pandemic we all had our faces stuck to screens a whole lot more than before. For many, in particular those with a predisposition for anxiety, this sets a strong foundation for the eruption of social anxiety. The more we disconnect, the easier we stay stuck to screens, the harder it becomes to break out of the cycle.

I attended a conference a few years ago that focused on screen addiction and while it was scary to hear all the facts, what was being reported made complete sense. Psychiatrists from all over the world stated that they would rather work with heroin addicts than screen addicts because of the neurological impact of screens. Social media usage can be seen as harder to address than drug or alcohol abuse because it's much more engaging and there's no social stigma attached to it. This makes treatment more difficult. Knowing how much I need to set boundaries on my *own* social media and screen time and how challenging that can be with apps that are designed to pull you in and keep you there, our kids have a minefield to navigate when it comes to being online.

Excessive screen use and gaming result in brains being in a constant state of hyper-arousal. While gaming, our brain doesn't distinguish between real and 'play' scenarios so the same stress cycle is created and the same stress hormones are released as if you were physically in the middle of whatever game it is that you are engrossed in. This skyrockets the likelihood of a person remaining in a constant state of fight or flight, even after they've finished gaming or spending time on a screen.

The fight-or-flight state can look different for everyone, but you might have noticed some of the symptoms below after your child or teen has had excessive screen time:

◅ More dysregulation, more meltdowns

◅ Irritability

◅ Higher levels of generalised anxiety

◅ More aggressive tendencies

◅ Depression.

Excessive screen time has also been linked to:

◅ Obesity

◅ Poor sleep and insomnia

◅ Impulsivity

◅ Lower social skills

◅ School difficulties

◅ Concentration challenges.

The other BIG issue in terms of resilience and connection-building is that when our kids and teens are absorbed in their screens, we have no idea what is going on inside their internal world. We may not know when the chaos within them feels so overwhelming that they are heading towards a pit of despair. We won't know what's happening in their peer relationships; we won't know when they are about to implode. We won't get to make memories in the everyday small and seemingly trivial moments of life that are so significant in building the strongest foundation for resilience. We won't know when they need support and if we don't pick up those little signs that we see when we are in one another's physical presence and engaged in connected family activities, then there's a dark rabbit hole waiting, filled with all sorts of things I as a parent do not want to contemplate for my child.

Make your own decisions about screen time, but be open-minded of the dangers, the impact on connection and consequently on a child's resilience.

'IT WILL NEVER ...'

Before you think that your kids and teens will never get sucked into the dangers of the online world, I should state that I have had countless parents weeping on my consulting-room couch saying the words, 'I never thought it would happen to my child ...' Anything is possible in the online world of gaming and social media. Be empowered knowing that what you learn and implement proactively in this area will make a huge difference.

DINNER TIME

Whereas screen time draws all of us away from family connection, there's a daily practice that does exactly the opposite. Some of the most overlooked yet powerful opportunities for connection can take place in the seemingly irrelevant times we spend together as families. Dinner time is one of those.

Here's my REALLY IMPORTANT question to you: Do you eat dinner together as a family?

This is an area that has been thoroughly researched and some people have written entire books on the benefits of eating together as a family. But here's the diamond, the fluff and all the major important benefits rolled into one: If you don't eat dinner as a family you risk missing some really important insights into your child's world.

Beware of making excuses like 'My partner gets home so late and the kids have already had dinner by then so we eat when they are in bed.'

Choose one meal to eat together. Make it happen. No excuses.

THIS is where things about their day surface – things that you would otherwise never know. In our rushed daily lives, for many of us this is often the first place we get to make proper eye contact with our children. It's often the first time (and only time) of the day that many parents and children connect.

It's often the first place where you become aware of any challenges they may have and if there are any issues that need to be looked into. If things are not going so well in their life, it's likely that you will realise this from the way they eat (or don't eat), their body language, the things they say (or don't say) and how they say them.

THE POWER OF TEN MINUTES

Studies show time and time again that when a parent takes just ten minutes a day to connect with their child, it has the power to turn the parent-child relationship around. Ten minutes of uncontaminated time free of anything, anyone or any kind of distraction – that's it.

Most days we run around feeling like there are just not enough hours in a day so asking for ten minutes can feel like a lot. It feels like yet another overwhelming addition to the daily to-do list and the 'box to tick if you want to be a good parent' list.

In our home when it starts to feel like all of us are about to break the dysregulation barometer, the sibling rivalry is a notch too high for my tolerance levels, or I've been the mom punchbag one too many times, I know the quickest and most effective way to turn things around is to find just ten minutes to connect one-on-one, distraction-free, with each of my kids. The logistics can be tricky when you have more than one child needing attention, dinner to serve and work emails hanging over your head, but those ten minutes are like an emergency band-aid when your relationship with your child or teen feels like it needs some extra, fast TLC. If you can't manage this every day, try every few days or even once a week. The most important thing is that your children are completely aware that the time is theirs, that it is sacred and not one minute of it can be touched by anything that will take away your attention. Not your phone, not your spouse, not their siblings, not the microwave beeping, not the kettle whistling – you are 100% theirs in those ten minutes.

We often try to control our children's play or guide the conversations with our teens, but PAY ATTENTION TO THIS: We need to enter into those ten minutes with ZERO expectations of what we will play or do, what our child's response should be, how the whole interaction should go down, how we are going to help them build the Lego or the blanket fort they've been planning. As much as possible and is reasonable, we need to hold our tongues and avoid any attempts at controlling any part of the interaction.

Your child or teen directs the play, *not* you. Let yourself be guided by them and do exactly what they want and need you to do. They choose the activity and they decide your EXACT role in it. Get out of your world and get into theirs.

EXPECTATION IS THE MOTHER OF ALL MESS-UPS

Expectation is a frequent slosh pit that we all stumble into at some stage. We walk into parenting and into interactions with our kids and we have expectations of what our children are meant to say, do,

PARENT EXPECTATION OF INTERACTION

REALITY OF INTERACTION

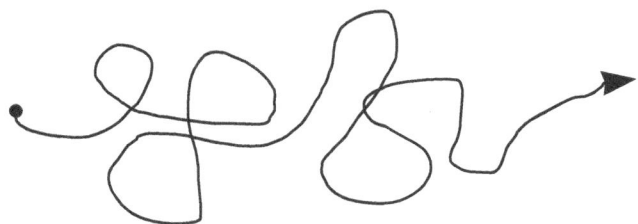

When our expectations are inflexible we become
disappointed and miss out on so many potential
moments of connection along the way!

or how lovely a time it's going to be together. Expectations lead to disappointment. They take away from 'what is' and turn our heads blinker-style to all that is not.

There's beauty in exactly what *is*, but we miss it completely when we are so fixated on who or what our child *should* be. The next time you interact or communicate with your child or teen for any reason, toss all the expectations. When we're able to do that, we open ourselves up to some incredible experiences that happen in moments of connection. It is in these times of zero expectations, when children don't feel pressured to be or behave in a certain way, when they don't feel that they have to be anyone other than exactly who they are in order to be accepted, loved and worthy human beings that the magic happens.

That is powerful groundwork for resilience right there.

≋ Attribute 13 ≋

'THE WAY YOU SPEAK TO YOUR
CHILDREN IS THE SINGLE
GREATEST FACTOR IN SHAPING
THEIR PERSONALITIES AND
SELF-CONFIDENCE.'
Brian Tracy

The words that we say to our children are reflections not of our children, but of OUR baggage.

How often do words come out of your mouth and you quickly realise that they had nothing to do with your child but all to do with your anger, your issues? Or something that you used to hear as a child? We pass more than our words on – we pass everything on, our body language and our tone of voice too. Our kids are so perceptive to those little things.

> 'SPEAK TO YOUR CHILDREN AS IF THEY ARE THE WISEST, KINDEST, MOST BEAUTIFUL AND MAGICAL HUMANS ON EARTH. FOR WHAT THEY BELIEVE IS WHAT THEY BECOME.'
>
> Brooke Hampton

What your children believe about themselves through the words that you say to them from the youngest age is what they become. And there's always more than one way to say things. Ask yourself if what you're saying, and how you're saying it, is building them up or breaking them down.

One Sunday afternoon when my son was about four years old, he wanted to make some pocket money so he asked if he could wash my car. Being a child who always wants to make some extra cash, always has a plan, and always has an entrepreneurial mind, he was so excited when I agreed.

I told him to go ahead. He was so proud of himself and took hours to wash it. Imagine a four-year-old with a sponge, a bucket, the hosepipe and a muddy (usually white) car. Enough said!

When he was done, he ran inside excitedly and said, 'Mom. Mom, come look. Come!'

I had been standing in the entrance hall taking a few photos because I was so proud of his fierce determination.

'Mom, look at your car!'

I could have said (and my first adult instinct *was* to say), 'What an awesome job, my love, but let me get the bucket and let's quickly sort these muddy stripes out.' But I stopped myself and instead I said, 'You have worked so hard on this, my boy. Thank you so much.'

He was as chuffed as chalk. Did it matter that my car had muddy streaks on it? No, it didn't. I just went to the garage the next day and got them to wash the windscreen so I could actually see out of it. What was so much more important was that he felt so proud of himself because he had achieved something.

THE POWER OF POSITIVES

The words we say to our kids make all the difference as to whether they feel good about themselves or not. Those words can break them down or build them up, and we need to think carefully before we speak.

Where is your focus in parenting? Is it on the 'cans' or the 'cannots'? Is it on what your children *can* do?

I always ask myself 'Does it *really* matter?' and I use this as a guide as to whether any behaviour really warrants a response. What have they done? What have they said? Does it really matter?

So often the things that we react to, the parts that we break down, that we criticise, that we judge within our children, don't actually matter. Our focus needs to be on the 'can' because that is how our child sees themself. It is easy to get into a repetitive cycle of only seeing the negative and I see this often with some of the parents who bring their kids to me for therapy. They only see the negative. The more negative you find, the more negative you will see. But at the same time, the opposite is also true. The more we notice the positive, the more positive we will see.

As a parent, I want to know that I have highlighted my son's and my daughter's strengths to them before the world shows them anything else or offers any other skewed perception of them.

Break that cycle and start to notice the positives, not highlight the struggles. No matter how 'foully' your children may seem to behave, there are always plenty of positives. It's useful to bear in mind that behaviour is never purposefully 'foul' – it really IS just a message.

MY SCHOOL-REPORT CONFESSION

 Disclosure: If you are the head of a school or an educator, please know that I was once an educator myself, who spent hours and hours typing up reports so I understand that what I'm about to say could be misinterpreted.

Here's my MOM-TRUTH: When those end-of-term reports come via email or via online access (and even when they used to come in those paper envelopes), I don't open them straight away. Why? Because whatever is written about my child is not as important as my relationship with them and no words in any report can ever equal the sum of the person my child is.

When my son was four his educator wrote a comment that he wasn't sitting still in class and was getting up too often to look at things that interested him around the class. Then the head of the school, who had never been into the class (great guy, but he'd never sat and observed my son for any length of time) wrote 'Doing well but needs to learn to sit still'.

I've read an obscene number of school reports in my line of work and I see this kind of copy-paste comment way too often from well-meaning heads who (understandably) do not have the time to closely observe a few hundred kids in their school so they end up skimming over what teachers have said and summarising it using their authority. In other words, they don't write anything. They sign the report and smack that oval school stamp at the 45° angle down in the bottom-right corner.

After that comment about my son, I hawk-eyed him at the dinner table and every time he age-appropriately shifted his bum in the chair, I said, 'My love, sit down. Sit still. Stop moving!'

I soon recognised the ridiculousness of the admonishment and gave myself a pep talk. He was doing what a child *should* do. He's not a robot.

My hawk eyes were a subconscious reaction to one tiny, unsubstantiated comment I had read, but our brains are capable of incredible focus even when it's unwanted (especially on the negative). At that moment, I decided I would never let someone else's words contaminate my connection with my children and determine my focus on their actions or my responses to them.

PS Again, educators, I appreciate the time it takes to finish reports. This is not personal; it is simply a personal boundary I have put up in the best interests of my relationship with my children. I also know that if there's an urgent issue requiring intervention, you'll call me in for a meeting. I have utmost respect for the incredible human beings in the teaching profession.

BELONGING

My little/big guy tends to struggle with his schoolwork. In his words, 'Mom, I don't like school but I love *my* school.' It's his way of saying that school work is hard, but he loves his school for so many more reasons than the academics. A really important factor in developing resilience, for anyone, is being in a space where they feel that they *belong*.

Let's for a moment go back to the analogy of growing strong roots in order for our children to develop resilience against life's storms. For these strong roots to grow, good soil is needed – soil in which *their* roots will thrive. When we are in the soil where we belong, we can set our roots down deeply, build strong relationships with our peers and gain a sense of worth and good self-esteem from how we perceive we are accepted by those around us. This cannot happen when we are in an environment where we feel that we are not fully accepted for exactly who we are and where we do not feel that critical sense of belonging.

A mom-lesson I have learnt through a lot of my own tears in recent years is that the soil your child is currently inhabiting may be everything YOU have always wanted for your child in terms of a school that embraces your home values, has fantastic invested educators and is everything you think is ideal for your child ... but maybe it's not right for YOUR child.

This doesn't mean that there is something wrong with your child or that the soil is toxic. A tree fern and a cactus are both beautiful and have the potential to thrive and bloom. They are also unique and require different habitats to root themselves in so that they grow to the heights of their possibility. Maybe the fit is wrong.

SCHOOL STRUGGLES AND RESILIENCE

If your child struggles at school, like both of mine do in various areas, it's even more important that you help them, through what you focus on, to see their strengths and talents in other areas and encourage them in those areas. They're seeing the world and themselves through your eyes, so work hard to help them always see the best first. This doesn't mean that your child never works on upskilling their weaknesses. In terms of academic challenges, your constant support of their difficulties – not judgement of them – and additional help such as extra therapies and remedial lessons may be essential. But what's more essential and critical for success and ensuring that your child maintains a healthy self-esteem despite these challenges is that *they* need to see their strengths first. Incidentally, weaknesses naturally improve when we focus on strengths (*#JustSaying*).

The standard education system tends to provide a very narrow view and, from the youngest age, children become acutely aware that 'intelligence' is measured by academic accomplishments, and that their value in a school system is only around sports and high achievements in academics.

Our children are *so* much bigger than that narrow perspective provides. Some schools are incredible in emphasising all strengths and focusing on holistic recognition of a child – from emotional intelligence (and attributes such as empathy and kindness) to cultural and technical strengths. Sadly, too many others are still instilling the conservative mindset that excludes the marvels of the brain and doesn't embrace all areas of our human development.

As parents we need to have discussions around different types of intelligence and strengths. My kids have always felt that they are 'different' and understood that they find certain aspects of school very challenging. However, they are equally aware that they have highly intelligent minds and, most importantly, kind and caring hearts. That, coupled with a sense of real belonging in their school environments, is what enables them to thrive regardless.

For the most part, they embrace themselves exactly as they are without comparing themselves to those around them. I was recently in the car with my son and we were talking about his incredible ability to always make a plan and to invent things. A few minutes later he piped up from the back seat, 'I like who I am, Mom.'

Silent mommy-tears welled in my eyes. THAT is all we as parents really need to know. That whoever our children decide *they* want to be (not who we decide they should be or who they become because of pressure from us and expectations to behave a certain way and be a certain way), they LIKE who they are.

It's never about our children's accomplishments; it's what they have to offer the world through becoming the people we see they can be. Through being the people they already are.

NOTICE THE 'WOW'

I wear a cheap plastic black band on my wrist alongside my watch. Although it used to have the word 'Forever' printed on it, that wore off a long time ago. I don't take it off because of what it symbolises to me. A while ago, my son took one of his coins and got the bracelet from a toy gumball machine. He ran up to me, handed it over and said, 'Mom, I wish it said "Forever Love", because I'll love you forever.' He just has that kind of heart.

He's also that kind of child who will collect every broken appliance that I toss on to the recycling pile, bring it back inside, fix it and put it back in the kitchen. A while back he came to me and said, 'Mom, I've got a problem. The light in my fish tank is not working.'

I said, 'Oof, that *is* a problem, my love.' My mind was racing knowing that there was no way I was going to get to the shops late on a Sunday to buy a new light for the fish tank before an impossibly busy week began.

Five minutes later, he called to me and said, 'Mom, come look.' I went into his room and he said, 'Moment of truth.'

He turned the fish tank lid upside down and there was a remote-control car motor stuck on with some tape and an elastic band. I had no idea what I was looking at, but again he said, 'Moment of truth.'

He turned the light switch on and the fish tank lit up! I was dumbfounded and said, 'My boy, how on earth did you do that? Honestly, it baffles my mind.'

He replied, 'I just thought that I would hotwire these wires with this little motor and kind of jumpstart it.'

I still don't understand what he did and I remain amazed at how his mind creates and makes and invents and, and, and ... It's up to me as a parent to see, notice and reflect my amazement in the 'and, and, ands'. It is up to me to see the 'wow' in my kids before the world reinforces a negative self-view due to anything that they're battling with.

Ask yourself this question, OFTEN: If your child saw themselves through your eyes, what would they see and what would they feel?

It's that simple, that hard and that true.

'YOU MADE ME SHOUT!'

We all shout, we all lose it, we're all human. After a stressful day at work we can all be triggered and become dysregulated, but if you recognise that losing your temper and shouting are more than once-in-a-blue-moon outbursts in your home, there are a few things you need to consider.

Shouting reeks of dysregulation and studies have shown that in households where there is a lot of shouting, children's self-esteem is negatively impacted upon.

We don't shout because of our kids' and teens' behaviour. We shout because we are dysregulated and cannot control OUR emotional space. We shout because we are stressed or haven't topped up our fuel tanks with that essential, daily self-care. Or perhaps we haven't remembered to breathe, or we are triggered because of our own childhood wounds that we haven't worked through.

You'll notice that not once have I mentioned the words '... because your child ... x, y or z ...' because this is about OUR stuff. No one else is responsible for our reactions. It doesn't matter if you've had the door slammed in your face, eyes rolled to the back of their sockets, food flung on your work suit or had a backchat comment hurled your way.

We choose how we respond. *Every. Single. Time.* When we do the self-work and make sure we are actively practising regulation and remembering 'It's not personal', then we can show up and be what and who our children need us to be in that moment.

Let me try and put this into perspective using an analogy from a situation I sometimes find myself in.

There is a single-lane, winding road heading up a hill that connects my residential area to my daughter's school. Some days perhaps I'm running a little late to do the school drop-off. Maybe I overslept. Maybe she couldn't get out of bed. Or maybe the school lunches took me a little bit longer than usual to put together. Or perhaps I remembered something last.minute.com as I was rushing out the front door.

But whatever it was, we are late and we are rushing. As a result, I am stressed and dysregulated and, as we hit that twisty, single-lane road, I end up behind a rusty, smoke-puffing, 30-year-old car that is incapable of going more than 30 kilometres per hour up the hill. It can't go any faster and I cannot get past it.

The red mist is rising within. My state of dysregulation is rapidly increasing. Heart palpitations. Shallow breathing. Knuckles turning white while brutally clutching the steering wheel. But the car isn't the problem; the car hasn't caused my flustered state, I have!

The next day I am driving up that same single-lane, twisty road on the way to fetch my daughter from school. It's been a brilliant day. I slept in a little that morning, the parenting load was shared, I had my morning coffee in bed while reading a chapter of my favourite book and then I treated myself to a pedicure and a massage before enjoying a late breakfast with an old friend.

As I'm heading up that hill, with half an hour to spare before my daughter finishes school, the SAME smoke-puffing, 30-year-old, rusted car pulls in front of me. It just can't go any faster, but it's okay. Today I have time. Today I am regulated.

It's the same situation, the same car, the same speed. The only difference is that because of my altered emotional space and regulation in that second scenario, I didn't have a meltdown and plummet into the pits of dysregulation.

It's not the situation or other people's behaviour that causes our reactions, the common denominator is us. It's the space we're in. Rather than feeling helpless about this, it is actually a GOOD thing. We can't change other people's behaviour; we can't control any aspects of life – not the 30-year-old car in front of us or our children's behaviour. But keep reading ...

THE PARENTING DOUGHNUT

There's a concept that's often used in psychology and life coaching called the circle of control. A variation of this was initially developed in the 1980s by Stephen Covey (an American educator, author, businessman and speaker) as a visual representation of the things in life that we have an influence over (circle of influence) and the things in life that we are concerned about yet can have little impact on (circle of concern). This original concept has been simplified over the years into the circle of control – simply identifying the areas in life we have control over and those we don't. This is a useful exercise as often so much of our mental energy is focused on things that we have no control over. When we make this into a visual diagram it becomes far easier to change our focus and let go of some of the stress we feel when we place our energy on aspects we have no power to change.

I call the parenting version of the 'circle of control' the parenting doughnut. It sounds more user-friendly and a whole lot more appealing.

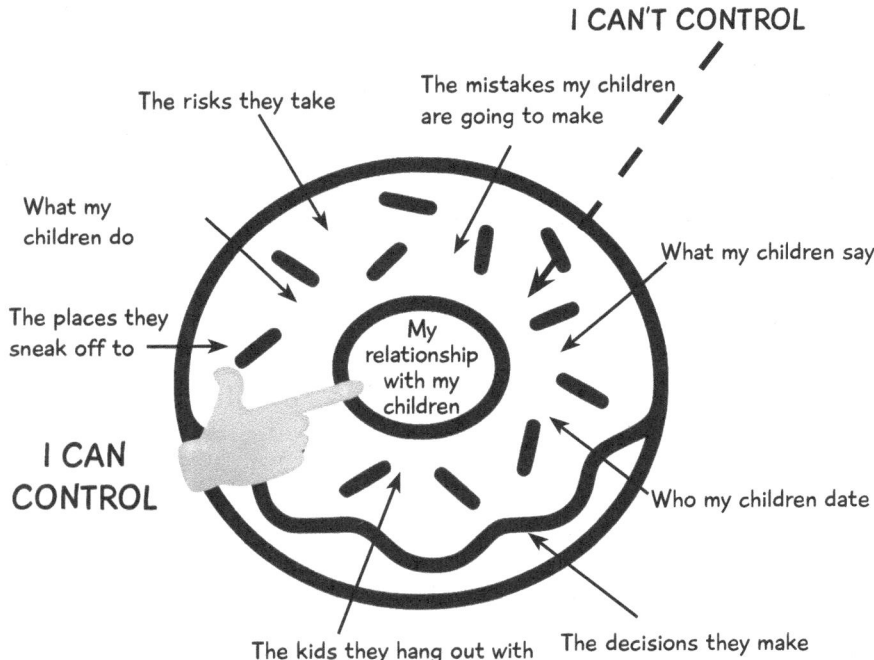

PARENTING DOUGHNUT

One of the hardest reality smack-downs of parenting is realising we can't control our kids and we shouldn't want to. No matter how big or little they are, sharing a few genes doesn't give us sole ownership rights. They are their own people.

We can't control what they say, what they do, who they choose to be friends with, the decisions they make, the places they go and the mammoth mistakes they *are* going to make.

That outer crispy part of the parenting doughnut? LET IT GO! Take deep, deep, deep breaths and let it go. None of those things in that outer ring is within your circle of control and focusing on them only leads to disconnection with your kids.

Re-centre and focus on the only thing you *do* have control over in parenting, which is your relationship with your child and teen. The words 'relationship' and 'control' should not exist in the same sentence. They contradict one another. A healthy relationship is an intricate dance between two people who want to be in it – no control, no force, no coercion.

Attempts to control are rooted in fear. There is *so* much out there that feels completely disempowering for us on this parenting journey and the temptation to forcibly take the reins is huge.

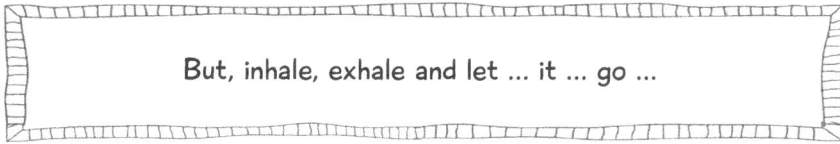

But, inhale, exhale and let ... it ... go ...

Whether you have a toddler or an adult child, the *only* factor you can control is YOU. You can control your responses, your words, your actions, healing your wounds and the quality and depth of your connection with your child and teen.

When you focus solely on the relationship and when the strength of the bond is in connection, you will always be the light-house. Your child *will* leave the safety of the harbour and they will venture out to stormy seas. And it's going to scare the heck out of you and you're going to want to hold them back and secure the ropes. But venturing out alone into rough waters is developmentally important for our kids so that they can separate from us and become their own independent selves. If you remain the consistent lighthouse, let go of the control and always focus on the relationship, that boat *will* return to the safe harbour ...

Do whatever you have to do (including not doing and not saying a whole lot that you may instinctively want to) to preserve and build your relationship.

Let that crispy outer ring go because focusing on it will tear your relationship apart. The seas are stormy, life is hard, so keep that light burning bright in that inner circle.

_____

_____

_____

_____

_____

_____

_____

_____

_____

CC Moment: Do I focus too much of my energy on aspects in life that I have no control over? What are things that take up a great deal of my mental energy that I need to work on letting go? Doing this will enable you to spend more time and energy on the most important aspect of building resilience within your child — your relationship with them.

21-DAY PARENTING GRATITUDE PRACTICE

Maybe you're thinking, 'You don't know my child, Naomi. I can't see anything good about them *or* their behaviour right now'.

I know that if you are reading this book, you are a concerned parent who wants to have a deep and connected relationship with your child. This exercise will take you less than five minutes a day and you can even do it from the comfort of your bed at night. Keep a little notebook next to your bed and every night reflect and write down three positive things you noticed about your child in the way they were that day. Not their accomplishments, not their 'good behaviours'. For 21 days, notice specific interactions and attributes that speak to the people they are.

Things like:

- ✓ You offered to help take the groceries inside without me asking.
- ✓ You tried hard to get your homework done without getting frustrated.
- ✓ You asked such interesting questions at the dinner table tonight.

Whether you decide to share these observations with your child, or keep your notebook for your personal reflections, you will notice an incredible shift happening within you as a parent and in your relationship with your child. When you can enter interactions or observe your child with zero expectations, you begin to recognise the amazing things about the human beings they are. Not the human beings you expect them to be or think they should be. Exactly who they are.

This can have a profound impact on their self-esteem and resilience because when you notice characteristics such as kindness, creativity, helpfulness and determination in them, that's how they will see themselves and value themselves as people who have an important role to play in this world.

Something powerful happens when you do this simple exercise, because the more you practise this, the more your mind automatically moves into finding the positive over the negative and the things that frustrate you about your kids. It can change that cycle of seeing the negative to becoming more and more aware of noticing and absorbing all the good that's always there. We sometimes just need to change lenses to see it.

The notebook can also become a precious memoir that you read and reread and smile every time you do. Read it to your kids every now and then. It's incredible how their faces will light up knowing that a parent has taken the time to NOTICE.

≋ Attribute 14 ≋

PARENTS OF RESILIENT CHILDREN ... ARE OPTIMISTS

How do you see the world? Do you see the light? Or is it all pretty much doom and gloom? Take a CC Moment to think about this because, depending on your answer, it may be something you need to do some work on.

_____

_____

_____

_____

_____

_____

_____

_____

I like to think children and dogs are natural optimists. When my daughter was a toddler and she first started speaking, her first word was 'Wow'. Everything was 'wow'.

Pizza arrived at the table – 'Wow!'

A donkey in the field – 'Wow!'

A moth against a window – 'Wow!'

But somewhere along the line, something happens. And that something is us. *We* happen.

Our children pick up on our space and absorb whether our response to the world, both verbal and non-verbal, is positive or negative. So are you a half-full or half-empty kind of person?

If you're the half-empty kind of person and see the world in a negative light, you can't expect your child to see it any differently. There's a correlation between optimism and resilience.

I'm not advocating a 'head-in-the-sand' ostrich approach. Optimistic parents don't ignore the dark. They see it but they choose to focus their attention and energy on the light and their children benefit in so many ways from the reflection of it.

When you are constantly focused on all that is going wrong around you – socially, politically, financially, in your child's educational institution – you are robbing them of their incredible capacity to see beauty and to feel joy. Our perspective becomes the filter through which our children see life.

When we can focus on the good that *does* exist in between all the darkness, we are role-modelling this perspective to our children. This plays a huge part in acting as an antidote to depression and it is a rewiring of neural pathways that IS achievable. We are far less likely to get sucked into a dark place when our brain is on autopilot to search for all that is right and good and beautiful in the world regardless of any other chaos.

To ensure that we are raising optimists who are able to see light even in the darkness it's essential that we are able to do that too.

Like all the other aspects of parenting, as I have said so often before – it starts with US. If you're wondering what you are communicating to your child, even through your non-verbals, in this regard, rest assured, they'll show you …

Our children are wired from the very youngest age to become similar to us. This is never more evident than when we see them mimicking us.

I bet I am not alone in this shocking revelation I had one day while driving on the highway. In my town, and along the highway stretch of it, there are *plenty* of trucks. Often inconsiderate ones. When my kids were still in preschool we were driving along, passing a truck, and my very young daughter leant towards the window and started jabbering at it in a very irritated voice, 'What are you doing?'

I remember swallowing hard and feeling quite stunned. I thought, 'Where is *that* coming from?' Closely followed by the realisation that it came from ME!

Our kids are role-modelling everything about us, including how positive we are about the world. Pessimism leads to depression.

Every day we make a choice. Every single day. We ride along the same mountain pass, but we choose which side of the window to look out of. Of course there will be days it's going to be harder to look at the sunny side, but we make that choice and our children see it.

KINDNESS JARS

Some kids are naturally more positive than others. It's just easier to rustle up their sunshine after any kind of cloud cover. Some children feel the world more deeply on an emotional level, take things more personally and tend to not always wake up on the best side of the bed.

Apart from negativity being utterly exhausting for everyone being exposed to it, the reason we need to shift what's happening in the brain is because negativity breeds depression and depression is the enemy of resilience.

Because of the brain's neuroplasticity, changes in thinking patterns, habits and behaviours *are* possible. As parents, it's our role to guide and nurture the growth process. We do this primarily through role-modelling (through our actions and attitudes) and guiding our children's brain circuits in the right directions. We do this in the way that we live every day.

We have some jars at home that I call kindness jars. Each of my kids has their own big glass jar decorated with their names on it. We have a little box of blank green and blue cardboard hearts that we get out for this exercise. Each evening after dinner, we take down their bottles. On a green heart my children write down one act of kindness that they did for someone else that day. On the blue hearts they write an act of kindness that someone else did for THEM. We date these paper hearts and pop them back into the bottles. (You can do this with your children from the youngest age. Let them relay what they noticed in their day and write it down for them.)

This creates a powerful mindshift to look for the positive in everyday life. It shifts the brain from seeing the negative to remembering the good that is everywhere and noticing the small acts of love and kindness that those around us dish out. Having the visual of the glass jar filling up plays a significant role in our children feeling worthy, valuable and lovable, and boosts their self-esteem. This is such a simple and practical exercise that gives our children (in fact, any of us) the ability to walk in the sunshine instead of living with our heads in that dark and thunderous cloud of doom and gloom.

ABOUT GRATITUDE

We hear the word 'gratitude' and get told to 'be grateful' so often that I think we lose sight of the psychological and physiological power of the impact of this word.

If you don't have a gratitude practice in your home, start one. It doesn't have to take lots of time, but the researched benefits of gratitude and the changes it creates in our thoughts, and thus our entire day, are astounding. Studies have shown that gratitude practices decrease levels of anger, anxiety and depression, elevate mood, improve sleep, ease chronic pain and increase immunity!

On the way to school in the car with my kids every day we each say something *specific* to that day that we are grateful for. 'Specific' is the key word, not some random and general 'I am grateful for my house' kind of thing. As marvellous as that is, it's so much more effective when we get mindfully present into the NOW and gratitude for what is NOW and TODAY.

Something like 'I am grateful for the sun shining through the car window this morning', 'I am grateful that we left on time and we can get to school early', 'I am grateful for my travel mug of coffee.' What's important is that whatever is said is done mindfully. This small exercise sets everyone's mind and mood in a good direction for the entire day and is like a knock-on domino effect.

~ Attribute 15 ~

PARENTS OF RESILIENT CHILDREN ... DON'T TAKE THE BAIT

This is such an important attribute, especially if you're moving into the tween and teen stages. Your children are going to throw ruthless comments your way and they may even throw actual objects your way. They will give you attitude, they will push back. They will be grumpy and they will be moody.

Your job is to take as many deep breaths as you need to and remember 'It's not personal!' In that moment of their lashing out, melting down, or whatever it is you are having to absorb, all they are doing is showing you a glimpse into their inner world. Something has unsettled them, something is making them feel unsafe, something is causing their nervous systems to go into a state of panic. Our tweens' and teens' brains at this stage of development are going through major renovations and overhauls (look back to Attribute 7) that further complicate things.

Every time you react as if it's personal and then become triggered, you've taken the bait. When you feel that red mist rising, inhale deeply and ask yourself, 'Can I let this one slide?' The cascading result of whatever your reaction is isn't going to be worth it. You're going to cause disconnection and a rupture in the relationship.

I know teens' behaviour can be so infuriating and feel so personal, but developmentally they are *meant* to be pushing our buttons and, by doing that, pushing us away. The role of a teenager is to become independent of their parents and a part of figuring out who they are is to give us the gears.

What we may view as 'negative' behaviour is for one of two reasons:

1. It's developmentally spot-on and an indication of what is meant to be happening in your child's body and brain.
2. They're struggling and having a really hard time with something.

The last thing they need is for you to be giving them a hard time too. Your child and teen's role is to show you what's happening in their internal world, one in which their brain and regulation system is still developing. You are the adult. Your role is to create that safe space where they can feel vulnerable enough to show you everything about their ugly side and know that when you have seen their worst, you are going to love them anyway.

DEALING WITH HARMFUL BEHAVIOUR

If your tween or teens' behaviour is harmful to themselves or others it is essential that you get the assistance of a mental-health provider as soon as possible in order to help them navigate the overwhelming emotional space they may feel that they are in. If your younger child is lashing out at others or hurting themselves, they're likely experiencing significant frustration, hurt, pain or shame and are struggling to regulate at that moment.

When harmful behaviour becomes a frequent occurrence, it is important to enlist professional support. If, however, this kind of behaviour is infrequent, immediately remove your child to a smaller room in which they will feel safer. In a calm tone of voice, make a statement such as, 'You're a good child having a hard time. I won't let you ...' Complete this sentence with whatever is appropriate for the situation. For example '... hit your brother, break the Lego, kick the dog' etc. Sit with them in that smaller, calmer space, or right outside the door. Never lock your child in a room or make them feel like you are sending them away from you for punishment or 'to think about it'. When your child has calmed and is more regulated, help them name what they are feeling and assure them that you'll hold the space for them. Repeat your assurance as often as is needed, 'You're a good child having a hard time and I am here to help you.'

HOW TO KEEP YOUR COOL!

Here's a quick guide as to what to do when you've been triggered:

- Notice what's happening in your body. You know you've been triggered as soon as you feel that 'red mist' rising.
- Breathe. Very, very deeply. Use one of the strategies mentioned in this book.
- Ground yourself. All you need to do in that moment is feel where your toes are. In your shoes? On the carpet? Focus your attention there for just a second.

◁ If that red mist is still resulting in a fiery blur, turn away, change positions or even get down on your knees. A shift in our brain happens when we move.

◁ Remember: (Yes, again!) This is not personal. 'My child is having a heck of a hard time, not giving me a ridiculously impossible time on purpose.'

◁ Ask yourself: 'What is the need behind this behaviour or is this developmentally appropriate according to their age?'

◁ Most often, some quick, compassionate connection once the raging storm has erupted does wonders for meeting our children's emotional needs and calming their nervous systems. It brings everyone back to a state of cooperation, which is where we ideally want to spend a maximum amount of time with our kids and teens.

◁ If you are really stuck, ask yourself, 'What's the kindest thing I can do for my child right now?' They are showing you what a difficult time they are having through their behaviour, so be kind.

◁ If you need to walk away, tell them you are stepping out to regulate yourself for a few moments so that you can come back and be who they need you to be. (I use the word 'regulate' often in my home and my kids have learnt exactly what it means.) By telling them what you are doing and that you are coming back, they won't feel like you are rejecting and abandoning them in their greatest time of need.

◁ Before you utter a word, take another deep breath. You are *not* a bad parent. You are a very human parent who is doing your absolute best to raise a human child in an upside-down world.

◀ When the chaotic moment has passed and you are both in your 'green zone' brain again, find a quiet way to connect and chat about what happened. Never blame your child for your emotional space or your reaction to their behaviour. That's on you!

◀ Do the couch work to untangle those triggers and up the self-care. That makes all the difference in those 'hot moments'.

You won't get these things right all the time (none of us do), but keep practising. Don't lose heart – remember that one degree at a time will land you on an entirely different parenting continent.

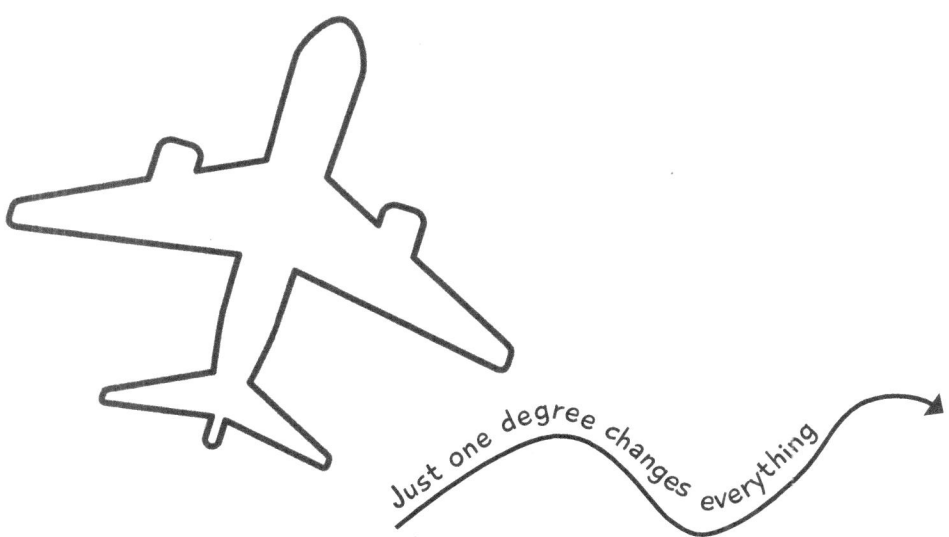

Just one degree changes everything

⁀ Attribute 16 ⁀

PARENTS OF RESILIENT CHILDREN ... ENCOURAGE PROBLEM-SOLVING

Our children are born as innately curious problem-solvers. Their brains make hundreds of thousands of connections every single second. When we jump in and try to fix and correct what we are doing is depriving our children from developing these abilities; we stifle them. We deprive them of the ability to learn how to problem-solve for themselves.

ANXIETY AND PROBLEM-SOLVING

Most anxious people are also highly creative problem-solvers, but in a state of anxiety that prefrontal cortex is stuck in survival mode and is not using executive functioning skills such as problem-solving.

Think about it like you're trying to remember a shopping list when you're being chased by that lion.

One of the things I always work on with anxious kids and teens is ways to bypass this 'stuck' state and access their problem-solving skills regardless. Developing and exercising these skills is really important when we are thinking about building resilience in our children.

TIPS FOR HELPING AN ANXIOUS CHILD ACCESS THEIR PROBLEM-SOLVING ABILITIES

If you have an anxious child and want to help them access their problem-solving skills when they're in a wound-up state, you're going to need to remind them of a few things:

1. Recognise what anxiety physically feels like in the body. This highly important first step is vital as we often feel the physiological impact of anxiety before we even realise that we are in any way worried. Some of these body clues may include butterflies in the tummy or even a painfully sore stomach, headaches, nausea, dizziness, rapid heart rate, fast and shallow breathing, shakiness and sweating. When those clues are recognised, move on to step 2.

2. Say either out loud or in your head: 'I am feeling anxious/ worried' or whatever other descriptive words come to mind to accurately describe your emotional space. When we name our emotions, we can begin to unlock that prefrontal cortex again and we are one step closer to accessing those highly creative problem-solving skills.

3. Do a quick grounding technique. This brings the anxious mind, which typically operates in the future or past,

back to the NOW. And in the NOW our brain enables us to breathe more deeply and our nervous systems feel safe. One of the techniques I teach is called the 3-3-3 rule. Name three things you see, three things you hear and then breathe deeply three times. This quick and simple technique can be very powerful.

4. By this stage, hopefully the nervous system will have geared down a few notches and your child will be able to come up with a solution to whatever problem they are facing.

PS These steps work fantastically well for all ages.
PPS If you're an anxious parent, there's a note just for you in the *By the Way* section (Part 3) of this book.

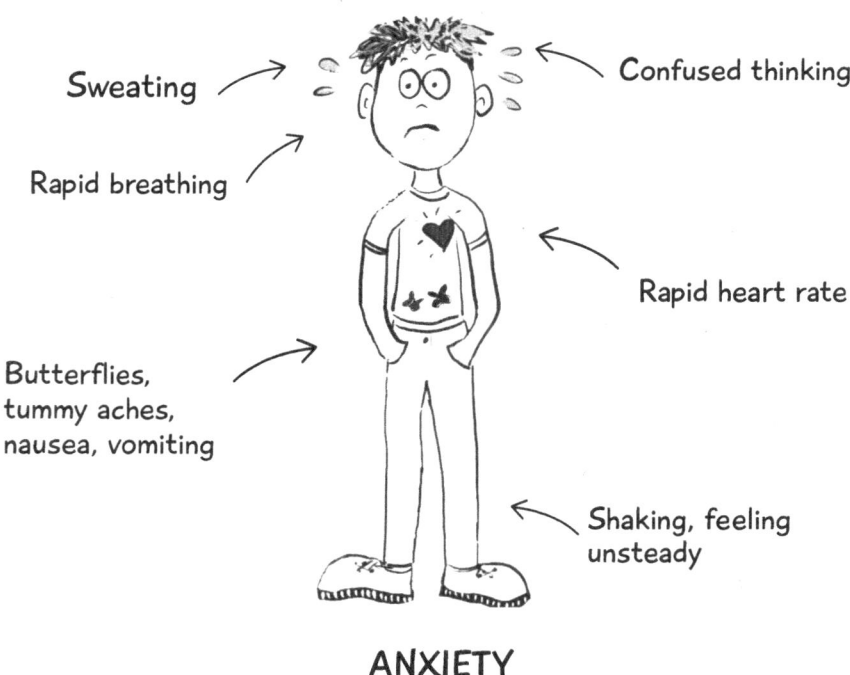

ANXIETY

When you're standing at the front door and you're ten minutes late for wherever you need to be and your child (who developmentally appropriately has zero concept of time urgency) is attempting to tie their shoelace, you really, really, REALLY want to get stuck in there and do it for them. Sometimes we do, but in so many situations we jump in way before we should. By doing that we're depriving our kids of learning that they *can* do things for themselves. They *can* come up with independent solutions, even if they take painstakingly long to come to this conclusion.

I always try to encourage my children to solve whatever problems they encounter and have always told them that they *are* problem-solvers. Sometimes they have had to remind *me* of this ...

 One afternoon when my little girl was about four years old, I was working in my home office and my kids were swimming (supervised). The next thing I looked up from my desk and my daughter was standing dripping in her wet cozzie and holding out a pair of cheap swimming goggles that I had bought her a few months before. They had snapped on the nosepiece and she very earnestly said, 'Mom, I've tried to fix these. Please can you help me?'

I looked at the goggles, knowing that they were way beyond repair and replied, 'My love, I don't know if we can ...'

She looked confused and said to me, 'Mom, but isn't it that Holdts can always make a plan?'

Although I had to tell her gently that this was one occasion that a plan *really* could not be made, a smile crossed my face. She had taken on board that no matter what the problem is, we have it within ourselves to always try to figure it out.

SUNDAY-NIGHT DINNERS

The way we parent can have a profound impact on our children's ability to problem solve. One of the many, *many* reasons I am such a fierce advocate of gentle parenting is because it enables us to raise independent thinkers, kind-hearted human beings and fabulous problem-solvers who are always eager to make a plan. I could relay many incidents that happen daily in my home that convince me of its benefits and the following story is just one of those.

My son loves making plans, helping people, finding lost items, inventing things – he is a true problem solver and, bonus for this mom, he has always had a good sense of what works flavour-wise in the kitchen.

It was a single-parenting Sunday and all day I had planned on making wraps for dinner. I had all the ingredients and the wraps 'were in the freezer'. Except they weren't. When I opened the freezer and my little/big guy peered in behind me sensing my sudden 'no-wrap' realisation, he piped up, 'Don't worry, Mom. I've got this covered. I'm making stew!'

And that's what he did. At his request, I didn't help at all – in fact, he didn't even want me in the kitchen! He defrosted the chicken, chopped the veg, sprinkled some spices, mixed a stock cube into boiling water and added a tin of coconut milk. It turned out to be a delicious dinner. He was thrilled with himself and the knowledge that he had made dinner for his family gave him a huge confidence boost.

Problem-solving and all other executive functioning skills and 'heart attributes' don't develop in a home where parenting is fear-based and authoritarian. When a child feels safe to be exactly who they are without the fear of judgement or punishment, that's when the brain grows. THAT's when the magic happens. That's when skills like this naturally develop.

WHY IS PROBLEM-SOLVING SO IMPORTANT?

If you want to add a little more to helping your child in this area, let's take a specific look at problem-solving and why it's such an important skill for our children to develop when it comes to resilience. If we can solve a problem, one that might otherwise have kept us knocked down and on the ground and disabled our 'bouncing-back' ability, then it's no longer a problem. Doing anything to attempt to solve a problem is motivating and gives us hope that a solution can be found if we keep trying.

There are many ways to help your child to develop this skill. The most important one is obviously role-modelling (there's that all-important word in parenting again). You need to be a problem solver who asks 'What can be done here?' and not lose your cool every time something goes wrong. You also need to have plenty of discussions with your child about situations you notice in the world around you and what can be done about them.

Everyday problems that can be discussed and solutions 'brain-stormed' with your child are things like:

- The neighbour's cat is lost.
- I want money to buy soccer cards.
- The SPCA needs winter blankets for the dogs and cats.
- I don't understand my maths homework.
- There is litter all over our local beach.

The key is to ask two questions: 'What's the problem?' and 'What can I do about it?'

The action of doing (or even attempting) the smallest thing when facing any problem shifts us from a disempowerment (steamrolled, I-can't-get-off-the-ground) state to an empowerment (I'm-trying-to-make-a-plan or I-am-identifying-that-a-plan-can-be-made-by-others) one ... and just like that, we are encouraging resilience.

THE PROBLEM-SOLVING TREE

Another way to teach problem-solving is to use the visual of a tree to assist your child (and yourself) to make decisions more easily. Problems and the resultant worries can leave us feeling very 'stuck'. I find this tool to be such a simple yet effective way to define problems and any life stresses and to gain a really clear picture of exactly how to move forward and 'unstick' from these. It works incredibly well for all ages!

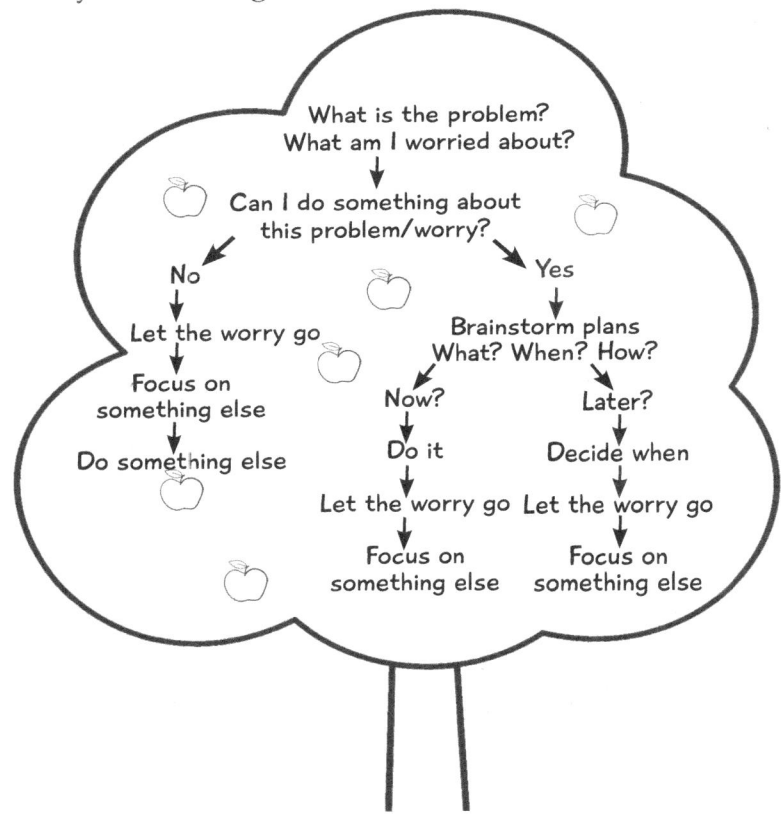

≋ Attribute 17 ≋

PARENTS OF RESILIENT CHILDREN ... EMBRACE A
GROWTH MINDSET

The terms 'fixed mindsets' and 'growth mindsets' were originally used by Carol Dweck, professor of Psychology at Stanford University. Our beliefs about growth and fixed mindsets, and what we practise within our homes, have a significant impact on our children and the mindset that they embrace towards life and their ability to develop resilience.

A fixed mindset is where we believe that aspects such as intelligence, talent, personality, character and abilities cannot change. People with this mindset tend to blame others, avoid risks and fear failure. They also tend to show a lack of effort in tasks and feel threatened by other people's successes.

A growth mindset is present when we believe that human beings are capable of change through practice and perseverance. When we can encourage a growth mindset in our children, they believe that with effort, they can improve in any area. Setbacks can be seen as opportunities and they can learn that success and failures are not tied to their identities. Wow! Can you see the impact that this mindset has on a child's resilience? Imagine a child believing, 'No matter how hard I am finding any aspect of life, and no matter how down I may be feeling, because I know that growth is possible and my parents have parented me to believe this, I know I can get back up, keep trying, and improve in all areas of my life'.

PARENTING WITH FIXED-VERSUS-GROWTH MINDSETS

I like to take the idea about growth and fixed mindsets a little bit further when I reflect on my parenting responses to my own children and the impact these are having on their resilience.

These thoughts are often powerful ones in stopping me in my tracks just before I may be about to react to my children's behaviour. They help me to take that breath and respond instead just a little bit softer before I react in a way that will bring disconnection.

Parents who have a fixed mindset react to children's behaviour in an attempt to curb it immediately and to stop the behaviour NOW because it is uncomfortable, frustrating, shameful or embarrassing. These parents often struggle to see 'the bigger picture' and do not understand that all behaviours are either developmentally appropriate or sending a loud and clear message about a child's emotional needs at the time. They tend to struggle with introspection and will have a hard time concluding that at times their children's behaviour, or their own inability to respond in a regulated way towards that behaviour, may just be because of a parent's own dysregulated emotional space. As a result, parents who feel the need to stop any behaviour immediately are more likely to try to control their children instead of reflecting on how their response can encourage future brain growth and benefit their children in the long term.

When we parent with a growth mindset, we respond to our child's behaviour by thinking about the impact of what we say and do in this moment on our children's future selves. We are remembering that our primary role as parents is to grow a child's brain, not turn them into mini 'yes sir, no ma'am' adults who will never reach their full potential because of our limited expectations. Parenting using a growth mindset and parenting to encourage a growth mindset means that we are parenting to raise caring, successful and more resilient children.

Situation: Child is having a meltdown in the shopping centre because they can't have a chocolate.

Fixed mindset parenting possibility A: Grab the chocolate off the shelf and give it to the child to stop the embarrassment of their screaming.

Fixed mindset parenting possibility B: Frustratedly tell the child that this is THE last time they are coming with you to the shops and there is no screen time for the next month!

Growth mindset parenting possibility: Take a deep breath. Own the fact that it's 4:30pm and, after a long day for both of you, it is not the ideal time to take a child to the shops. Make a note to pack a healthy snack for the car before arriving at the shops next time or not bring the child with you (if at all possible). Tell the child something along the lines of 'I can hear how much you want that chocolate right now and I know that your body must be very hungry. You can absolutely have a chocolate another day. Right now let's go choose a sippy yoghurt or find a banana that you can snack on until dinner time.'

This scenario could be adapted to apply to children and teens of all ages. It may not always go down as smoothly as that, but in parenting with this growth mindset we are taking on board that curbing a behaviour RIGHT NOW often leads to disconnection and is not helping brain development at all. When we pause to focus on connection and respond as calmly as possible, we are helping the brain develop the ability to regulate (upper-brain skill), to learn delayed gratification and to creatively embrace alternative solutions in situations where we cannot have what we want right away.

It's a no-brainer. Resilient children have growth mindsets and parents of resilient children focus on developing these within themselves and through their own responses to their children.

MINDSET MESSAGES

Our words and actions give children, from the youngest age, a message about how to think of themselves and their abilities. Often, unintentionally, we 'fix' our children's ideas about their capabilities through the unconscious messages we send them. Children are very perceptive to these messages and, as I see so often in my practice, become very anxious when they fear letting their parents down, not living up to their expectations, or feel exceptionally judged by their parents.

When children are raised in homes where parents embrace fixed mindsets they feel as if their 'success' in any area is always being measured. This leads to a significant amount of anxiety, stress and an environment in which resilience is very challenging to develop.

To teach our children to have growth mindsets we need to actively work on having these ourselves in every area of our lives. As we have read several times in this book already, our children learn far more about life through how we live and who we are than through what we say to them.

HOW TO ENCOURAGE A GROWTH MINDSET

Be a life-long learner:

- ✔ There are few things that I find more frustrating than having a conversation with a 'know-all'. We are all scholars on a journey with the potential to learn every single day. The fact that you are reading this book and putting what you can into place to grow and nurture your relationship with your child says that you embrace the growth mindset — a recognition that we are all capable of changing and have unlimited potential to be our best human selves and our best parenting selves. On the basis of that, I am going to step out there and say that you can tick this box already!

- ✔ Parent for the future. Remember: We need to parent, not by controlling behaviour **NOW**, but to develop neural pathways that will help our children's brains develop the qualities they need to become emotionally healthy and resilient adults.

- ✔ Talk to your children about the amazing power of their brains to grow and learn. The brain is a muscle that has the potential to keep growing forever. (Thank goodness for neuroplasticity, which means we can generally change and develop any aspect of ourselves that we consciously pay attention to!) Just like going to the gym to get the biceps we want, we need to practise and exercise our brain muscle for it to grow. When we do that there is no limit to what we can learn or accomplish in life. How amazing is **THAT** thought!

- ✔ Have daily discussions with your child that encourage them to think about how their brain grew that day. In my home we often do this at dinner time by asking the simple question: What did you learn today?

More growth mindset questions:

✔ What did you try hard on today?

✔ Did you ask for help today? Who helped you? How did it make you feel?

✔ Did you show kindness to anyone today?

✔ What challenging task did you attempt today?

✔ Was there anything you could have tried harder at today?

✔ What happened today that made you keep going even when it was difficult?

✔ What problem did you solve today?

✔ Role-model perseverance and effort. This is a CC Moment to ponder over: Do your children see you trying to problem solve and keep on going even when a task is super hard? They learn the skill of getting back up and keeping at it from us.

_____
_____
_____
_____
_____
_____
_____
_____

✔ Encourage risk-taking and failure. People who struggle with anxiety will often not attempt a task at all so that they don't have to risk failure, rather than try it and recognise that success is possible. If we don't try, we don't know and we can't grow. From the youngest age, talk in your home about how failures are learning opportunities. Be very aware of how you talk about the failures and setbacks of others and of your own. If a child feels that we judge or criticise others for their mistakes, they certainly won't feel comfortable enough to try anything new and risk failing in front of us.

✓ Talk about people in history who have struggled, failed, kept trying and experienced success. When talking about success, talk about HOW a person achieved it through hard work, consistent effort, trying multiple times, changing ideas, problem-solving, rethinking solutions. We do this so often in our house. My son, the constant inventor, frequently has to rebuild his various creations numerous times before they work (and sometimes the original plan doesn't work at all and requires plenty of adjustments). We use these opportunities to reflect and chat about the many 'greats' who had to make so many mistakes along the path to success, but that each mistake was a learning curve and one step closer to a brilliant result. You can do some googling that suits your situation, but the names we often talk about in our home include Thomas Edison, Albert Einstein, Henry Ford and the Wright brothers.

✓ Model positive affirmation talk/statements. It's a good exercise to make a note of all the internal thoughts you say about and to yourself every day. I often use the analogy of 'Imagine your best friend was with you 24/7 and said the things to you that you say to yourself about yourself. At the end of the day, would you still want to be their friend? And how would you be left feeling?' Too often our thoughts about ourselves are very critical and judgemental (and reflect a fixed mindset). So instead of them being compassionate ('You can do this. Keep trying!') they tend to be harsh ('You stupid twit. I can't believe you turned down the wrong street!'). Turn those thoughts around and be as compassionate and patient with yourself as you would be to a good friend.

✔ Talk through problems and encourage children to think of solutions. Attribute 16 discusses in detail how to help your children build problem-solving skills. In terms of a growth mindset, this is a super-important aspect. I even use car trips to ask questions to get my kids thinking in the 'enquiry and problem-solving mode'. For example, if we pass a truck stopped on the side of the road, I will casually ask questions like, 'Do you think that truck is broken down? What do you think the problem could be? If you were broken down on the side of the road, what would you do about it?' There are countless situations that you pass as you drive, as you walk through shopping centres and even around your home that encourage problem-solving when you start asking questions. My kids love this game and I am always amazed at the answers they come up with. But what am I teaching their brains? When a problem arises, we don't give up. We think about what could have caused it and then come up with a few solutions. Woohoo! Growth mindset development happening right here!

✔ Don't only praise children for their accomplishments. We've chatted about the risks of doing this in previous attributes, but it can't be emphasised enough. It's so easy to focus on the 'wows' and 'well dones', on what is visible to the external world and what reflects well on us as parents. An A on a report card. First-team rugby. Talent. Talent is fixed and when a child believes they either have it or don't, it can really leave them feeling beaten to the curb when they don't 'measure up' or when they mess up in some way. As awesome as skills and accomplishments may be, what we need to be encouraging and focusing on are attributes like perseverance — on the whole child — not just sports and other visible achievements. We want our children to believe that they are capable of anything and just because they may not have come first in Science or had a podium gala finish, there is nothing holding them back from getting there.

YOUR MINDSET MATTERS

Your child has endless potential to accomplish whatever they would like to in any area. Your beliefs about them and the mindset in which you parent them play such a significant role in their self-esteem, the person they will become and their ability to bounce back from the knocks that life will throw at them. As with all aspects of parenting, work on your own mindset first. This will have the greatest impact on your ability to help them develop theirs.

FIXED MINDSET

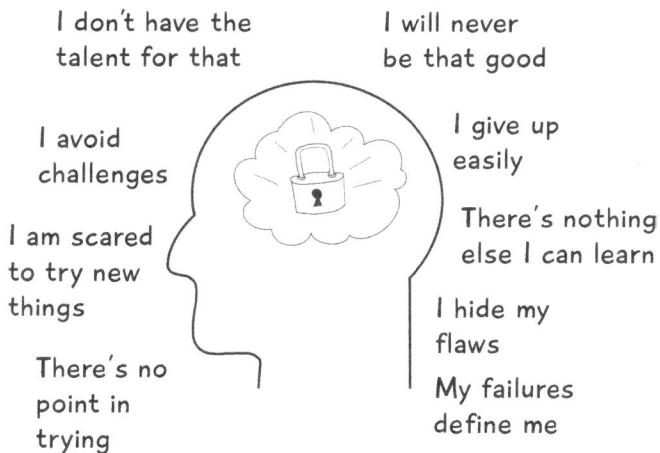

I don't have the talent for that

I will never be that good

I avoid challenges

I give up easily

I am scared to try new things

There's nothing else I can learn

There's no point in trying

I hide my flaws

My failures define me

GROWTH MINDSET

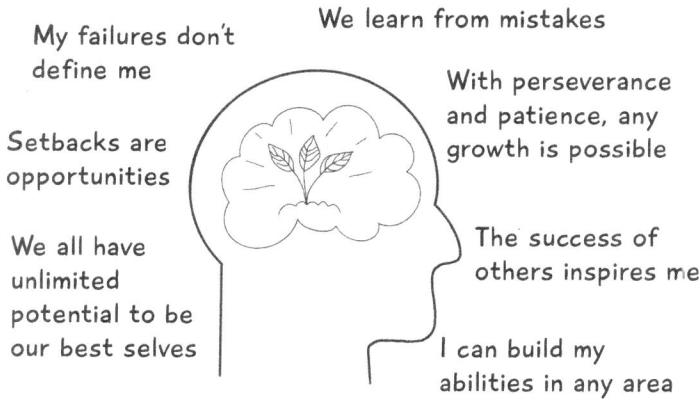

My failures don't define me

We learn from mistakes

Setbacks are opportunities

With perseverance and patience, any growth is possible

We all have unlimited potential to be our best selves

The success of others inspires me

I can build my abilities in any area

≋ Attribute 18 ≋

PARENTS OF RESILIENT CHILDREN ... CAN 'LET GO'

When we fail to support our children towards independence, we are assisting their 'failure to launch'. As hard as it is for some of us moms, in particular, to let go, our kids will never find their wings and take off in the direction they need to when we are clipping those wings, running behind them and, without even realising it, giving them the message, 'Don't fly! It's not safe! Stay close to home!'

I see so many kids, teens and young adults who are depressed and anxious because their parents aren't letting them go. There's too much 'cotton-wooling' happening. It's challenging letting our kids head out without us and it's especially hard for parents to let go and trust that their children are going to be okay when there has been any kind of past trauma in their own lives – medical or otherwise.

There is a direct correlation between independence, anxiety and depression. The child who hasn't developed independence becomes the adult who feels too unsafe to let go. They believe that there is no way they will cope in the world by themselves because we haven't allowed them to see otherwise. We haven't stood back long enough to watch them fall and then supported them from the sidelines while they found their way back up and realised all by themselves that they could keep going. We jumped in at the first sign of our kids toppling.

It's human instinct, I know, but part of helping our kids to independence so that they can feel resilient is creating a space where they feel safe enough within consistent boundaries to explore, to try things out and not be afraid to collide with the ground while they learn.

Think about a situation like teaching your child to ride a bicycle. If you keep holding the back of that bicycle and stabilising it, your child is never going to learn to ride. *You* have to be brave enough to let go and by doing that you are giving them the message that you trust that no matter what happens, they're going to be okay. Your actions are telling them that you believe in their ability to learn and achieve without you. You are giving them the freedom to grow and enabling them to experience the happiness that can only come from a powerful silent inner sense of 'I CAN do this. All on my own'. No child can mature into an emotionally healthy and happy adult if they still feel that they need a parent in order to succeed, in order to survive any part of the world 'out there'.

It's natural for us to want to hold on to our kids for as long as possible and it's the hardest thing to trust that when they are out of our sight, they *will* be okay.

> Holding on is holding back.
> As parents, we need to step back, hold the safety of the boundaries and watch our children fall and scrape their knees. Somehow, when they know we are watching from a distance, but not rushing in, they believe that they can get up and they do.
>
> That is one of the most valuable gifts we can give our children. The knowledge that we believe in their ability to grow and their capacity to go on to live happy lives without us. Ultimately, that's our role as parents — to raise kids who go into the world and flourish.

 I recently hand-raised a hadeda chick that had fallen out of its nest during a huge storm on a friend's farm. His parents did not return for him by the next day, so obviously we took him in. For the first month, Happy (as we called him), slept inside the house in a warm, blanket-lined box and I syringe-fed him a blended mixture of pricey, soft cat food, soaked cat pellets and sometimes even some mealworms mixed in.

Without ever intending the over-reliance, Happy imprinted on us and even though he progressed to sleeping outside and on our rooftop, he still flew down daily for his syringe feedings. Knowing we were leaving on holiday and that there would be no one to feed Happy, and also knowing that he was in fact old enough to be fending for himself, I decreased his feeding to twice a day. He spent his days poking his long beak into holes in the garden and I'm sure he must have found some bugs to eat, but I *still* worried about the little thing.

Eventually, two days before we were due to leave on our two-week getaway, I called FreeMe, a wild animal rescue centre in the area. I explained the situation to a kind lady at reception and she said to me, 'Ma'am, it sounds like you have done a great job raising him. Happy's mother would have kicked him out of the nest by now. Sometimes you have to be cruel to be kind. That's what his mother would have done.'

While I'm not suggesting cruelty of any nature, this lady reminded me that sometimes the kindest thing we can do to help our children reach their potential and to actually thrive is encourage them to leave the nest. Sometimes we have to give them a little bit of firm nudging.

That's what we are raising them for. Not to still be in our nest at 40 years old. We raise our kids to leave the nest. They're happiest when they find their own. You don't have to worry that once they leave they will never come back. If your focus has been on creating a good relationship with them they'll always find their way back home for 'check-ins'.

I often see children with a 'failure-to-launch' issue (which can happen at any age of a child's life when they are held back from where they are meant to be emotionally) when there are problems in a marriage. In these cases, parents present the child as someone who can't let go, that is too dependent on them, yet it's the *parent* who cannot let go of the child and face the issues that need to be addressed between them and their partner.

Our children need to believe that after those inevitable knock-downs in life, they can get up and they can keep going and keep trying. We are not always going to be there and our kids and teens will become depressed and anxious young adults if they don't learn that it's something that they can do on their own while in the safety of our care.

Walk your own journey and let your child walk theirs.

It is a huge disservice to our children to make them so reliant on us that they are incapable of leaving us.

Attribute 19

PARENTS OF RESILIENT CHILDREN ... ALLOW THEIR KIDS TO 'MESS UP'

My kids both had the same incredible Grade 1 teacher. She is a phenomenal woman and educator for many reasons, but one of the vital life skills she reinforced, one that we constantly talk about in our home too, is mistakes.

Within the first week of Grade 1, both of my children bounded into the house saying, 'Mom, guess what? Mistakes are good. We learn when we make mistakes.'

I'm so thankful that there are educators like her who reaffirm this truth – mistakes *are* the best opportunities to learn.

I firmly believe that we could all benefit from pyjama days (aka mental-health days). When I sense that my kids need one, I let them take a day off. On one particular occasion, when my daughter was about four years old, she came into the kitchen, still in her pink pyjamas, and announced that she wanted to make her own lunch. She wanted Marmite toast. I watched from the sideline as Little Miss Independent toasted the bread and buttered it. She was insistent that she would do it all herself. And then came time for the Marmite. Now, if you are a Marmite-eater you will know the unspoken Marmite rule that you spread the thinnest layer, just touching the uppermost corners of the bread. Not my little girl. She loaded it on and of course, one small bite into her Marmite-laden piece of toast, she decided she wouldn't be eating any more of her bitter-tasting lunch.

If I had stepped in that day, halted the over-loaded Marmite process and insisted on doing it for her, she would never have learnt the importance of 'less is more', especially in the case of certain sandwich spreads. It's also highly likely that she would have been infuriated with me for undermining her attempt at independence and the 'headbutt' would have resulted in a certain disconnection between us.

Needless to say, the Marmite toast went into the dustbin that day and her preference for Bovril has remained, but she learnt because she made her *own* mistake.

I recall another learning-through-mistakes moment made by my little girl at around the same age. She decided that she wanted to bake her own cupcakes from her *own* recipe. (I think my leniency in the kitchen is as a result of doing this myself as a youngster and then torturing my family by insisting that they taste my not-always-so-tasty baked goods.) With the help of her then six-year-old brother, they wrote out her recipe. It had all the basics:

2 cups of flour

1 egg

2 teaspoons of sugar

$\frac{1}{2}$ cup milk

... but it was missing a key ingredient ...

If you'd seen the cupcakes, you would have noticed how incredibly flat they were. Everything else was perfect and they tasted delicious (especially since they were loaded with rainbow sprinkles) but they were flat. She had forgotten entirely about the baking powder.

I saw this all unfolding in the kitchen and I could have leapt in and said, 'Whoa, guys, that recipe is going to flop. Stop right there, let's fix it.' But then they never would have learnt that if you want big vanilla cupcakes, you need to add baking powder.

Our kids learn through us allowing them to make mistakes and not jumping in to fix them. They need to know that within the boundaries, the safe boundaries you as Mom, Dad or whoever's looking after them put up, they are safe to make mistakes and can get back up again.

Not too long ago I was reminded of the perfection of our imperfect humanness.

I was tidying the kitchen, probably in too much of a rush, as often happens, and the glass pepper grinder slipped out of my hands and smashed all over the kitchen floor, shattering into hundreds of tiny shards and slipping into the grooves of the floor tiles. My eight-year-old daughter walked in and quietly, yet assuredly, stated:

'It's okay, Mamma. We all make mistakes.'

Her words made my mom-heart smile and in that moment I hoped that her heart would always believe them. I know that my little girl understands compassion and embraces it completely.

Mistakes are what we do in our house. We do mess-ups. We do yell-ups. We do clean-ups. We take the wrong paths. We make faulty decisions and some days we completely stuff up. But we also do 'sorrys'. We do hugs. We do compassionate forgiveness of ourselves and one another, and we clean the glass fragments out of the grooves of the kitchen tiles together. By dealing compassionately with the mistakes that we make, and the ones that every other family member makes, I am attempting to model the compassion and forgiveness that I hope my son and daughter always treat themselves with.

Life is full of mistakes. We *are* all going to make them. Some days we're going to submerge ourselves in their carnage. Any attempt to maintain an exterior appearance of perfection and pretend that the mistakes don't happen 'in our homes' only creates anxiety and leads to disconnection.

When we don't own these mistakes and talk about them with our kids as though they are everyday normal events, our children grow up believing that mistakes are intolerable. I grew up in a home where all mistakes were punishable and many kids and teens I see in therapy (and adults I work with) have similar experiences.

Unless we are very comfortable with our own human selves as parents, our insecurity can lead to our children feeling like mistakes shouldn't be made. This is reinforced when, despite a shift to the more 'real' on social media, so many people continue to only post a picture of 'perfection'. Our kids and teens are absorbing this and it leaves them feeling 'less than' too often.

Reframe mistakes; they are an inseparable part of the beauty of our imperfect humanness.

The one place in the world where we want our children to know that they can make mistakes and feel safe enough to do that is within the safety of our homes and with the support of our unconditional love. This is where they need to learn to try, to experiment and to unashamedly make mistakes as a part of their very human journey of learning to navigate life.

Attribute 20

PARENTS OF RESILIENT CHILDREN ... SAY 'I'M SORRY'

Saying sorry is one of the most important things that we can do for our kids. Many of us were raised in homes where parents never said they were sorry. My parents *never* said the word. I never heard that phrase.

If something's wrong and children are sure they didn't do anything or have no idea what they could have done, yet parents aren't saying sorry, then children presume it must be them who is at fault. They internalise the bad, define themselves as bad, as worthless, as not good enough, and as constantly needing to try harder.

This cycle is a fertiliser for depression and anxiety that is spread when we don't offer a sincere apology. Saying sorry is a gift to our children because it gives them permission to be human too. We cannot connect to perfection.

_____

_____

_____

_____

_____

_____

_____

_____

_____

Take a **CC Moment.** If your parents never apologised to you as a child it's likely that you will not have had the deepest or closest relationship with them because they will never have been able to be vulnerable enough with you to deeply connect.

THE GIFT OF HUMANNESS

I am a mom who is very far from perfect and who says 'I'm sorry' often. One evening I was dysregulated and in frustration I shouted at my daughter. As the words came out of my mouth, I knew I was going to need to do some repair work. Riddled with guilt, I softly said to my daughter, 'My darling. I am so, so sorry. I should never have shouted at you. I was wrong. I need to work more on regulating myself.'

She was seven years old at the time and threw her arms around me and said, 'It's okay, Mamma, you're just human.' It brought tears to my eyes. Her compassionate forgiveness of my human state was immediate and it brought such comfort to know that, even at her young age, she has embraced that it's okay to make mistakes. She knows that if her mommy messes up and says sorry, she can mess up too. In terms of resilience, a child who knows that they can make mistakes and be forgiven, no matter what, and forgives others who may have knocked them down, is a child who can get back up after the knocks.

On the occasions I have needed to apologise to my kids not once have they said 'That's it, Mom. That's the final straw!' Instead they usually throw their arms around me, pull me close and hug me tight.

Giving your children permission to be human is one of the best gifts to give – the permission to be fallible, to be imperfect, no matter how much of a superficially picture-perfect world we live in.

When your children and teens are older and they make big mistakes, they'll know that they can come to you and you can guide them through whatever may have happened because you are not perfect either. For me that's an incredibly comforting truth.

THE GIFT OF MULTIPLICITY

We all have bad days and on those bad parenting days we need to compassionately remind ourselves of a few things. One of them is that there are NO bad kids. Our kids are good kids who on those not-so-good days are having a hard time. That's how we need to see those days and that's what we need to communicate to our children. 'You're a good kid having a hard time.' When we can't do this, our children internalise that they ARE bad.

We also need to tell ourselves over and over again that we are not bad parents. We are good parents having a hard time.

We need to have grace and compassion for ourselves. Our kids will not learn to have compassion for themselves when we are hard on ourselves. If we lack compassion, the inevitable result is walking around with that burdensome yoke of feeling 'not good enough' and that so often goes hand in hand with depression and anxiety.

If we can't feel good enough and constantly beat ourselves up for not being good enough, we can pass this mindset on to our children.

As parents we always believe that we have to do more, be more, but then end up filled with resentment, burnout and are not able to show up for our kids as they need us to.

Quite some time back, when our household was in the midst of our 'sangry' phase, it had been a particularly bad single-parenting week. One of my children had been dealing with some really hard things in their life and the two of us had *the* almightiest fall-out. A very pear-shaped evening turned to rotten fruit salad. 'Horrendous' is the only word that comes to mind.

After a few hours we ended up hugging, crying, and saying our 'sorrys' to one another. We eventually both went to sleep, but the next day I felt like someone had taken me and grated my soul. I felt so raw and so vulnerable.

I gave myself a harsh and critical internal lashing, 'How can you be so passionate about parenting but disconnect so badly from your child? That was not good-enough parenting. You should be doing better'.

I vividly recall, towards the end of that soul-destroying day of my harsh inner critic tearing me to shreds, as I was driving home and I suddenly put it all together. Another voice inside my head began a counter-argument. 'Stop it. Those harsh words are not mine'. I thought long and hard about where they were stemming from because I knew that when I could figure that out, I could begin to be less harsh with the self-blame.

And guess where they came from? That voice that had bellowed that I was 'not good enough and that I could do better' came from growing up in a home where things were all or nothing. You were good enough or you were terrible. You got an A symbol or you failed. You came first in a race or it was nothing to talk about.

As parents we need to embrace multiplicity as an idea of perfectly okay varying perspectives. I can be a phenomenal parent *and* have a bad parenting day. I can love my kids to pieces and want to spend time with them and also have days where I want to jump in my car, drive to the airport and fly away. That doesn't make me a bad parent, it makes me human.

I was able to realise that the reasons I was torturing myself were not based on any kind of reality. Despite all my parenting imperfections and the many mistakes I make, I *am* a good parent. That harsh inner critic stemmed from my childhood wiring. Only when I could understand the origins and reckon with that inaccurate inner voice was I able to be compassionate with myself. We all have to learn to do this and it's probably something that many of us will have to continue to work on.

You've journeyed your way through this parenting book and maybe filled the pages with funky reminder notes. You're an invested parent. A committed parent. A fallible parent who is doing everything within their power to raise a happy and resilient child. That makes you MORE than average and so much more than good enough.

> You're allowed to have bad days. Those days don't define who you are as a parent; they just mean that you're human. And your kids need to see that too.

WHAT ABOUT GRIT?

So many people ask me, 'How do I build grit within my child?' Some people spend thousands and thousands on programmes teaching themselves and their children to develop grit. But here's the thing: grit doesn't develop in isolation. Grit develops in the context of loving relationships.

Grit develops when a child feels safe within an environment where deep connections exist. Because of those deep connections, they allow themselves to be more vulnerable, to open themselves up to possibilities, to extend themselves and grow. They feel safe enough to fall, scrape that knee and get back up and keep going.

That is grit. It's keeping on going.

WRAPPING IT UP

At the beginning of this book I said that it's likely you may only remember three things (although I'm hoping that you remember many more!). Which three stuck out the most for you? Go and do those first.

You can start building resilience and a stronger foundation for resilience from the second your child wakes up tomorrow morning. (Although I am sure that while you have been reading these pages, you have already started doing exactly this!)

Resilience is not the complex topic that so many make it out to be. At the heart of it is always, always ... (complete the sentence because I know you know the answer by now) ...

CONNECTION

The most important determining factor for building happiness and resilience is connection. There have been many days when, in the chaos of the overwhelm, feeling empty of any ideas to save a particular situation, I have opened my arms and invited my children into my embrace. That's all I could offer and it was enough. To quiet. To calm. To reconnect.

When you don't know what else to do, just be. Quietly, wherever you are.

Most parents I know are in a constant state of exhaustion, but it's the small things that become the strongest foundations of connection with your children. Building resilience is not about teaching skills. The qualities that make up resilience develop naturally within the safety of a deeply connected relationship. That's where your focus needs to be.

You cannot know what will happen in your child's life in ten or 20 years' time, what obstacles they will encounter, what losses they will endure, what hardships they will need to overcome. But you *can* know that what you do right now makes a difference to how well their future selves will survive, whatever comes their way.

PART 3
By the Way

Dear Anxious Parent

I was one of you. In truth, I think at times we all are. My childhood wiring predisposed me to anxiety and parenting increased that exponentially.

It took me a while to realise that I was fast becoming THAT parent. The one who parented in fear – the fear of complete parenting failure, the fear of recreating the cycle of the home I grew up in, the fear that judgement would be dished out by all and sundry, the fear of losing my little beings – the other part of my heart – the ones who first breathed within, and then outside of my body.

This fear began before my son was even born. As his due date grew closer, I remember having the conversation with my gynaecologist about whether I wanted a natural birth or a C-section. All I wanted was a healthy, alive baby, so I asked her, 'What is the safest way to get this baby into the world? Nothing else matters.' And right then, before I even met my son face to face, that fear began regulating every one of my parenting decisions.

Anxiety cripples us. It cripples our children and our relationship with them. And because it keeps us trapped in the past and the future – ruminating and worrying – it keeps us far, far away from the now. It's like a palisade fence between us and our kids. We can see them and we have all the best intentions of connecting, but we just can't quite get there and there seems to be a whole lot of spikes in between.

When we parent in fear, we can't grow. Our relationship with our child can't grow. We make the wrong decisions simply because we aren't able to use our prefrontal-cortex skills when we are in a state of fear.

Our children can't breathe when we are parenting anxiously and the whole process becomes stifled. A plant without oxygen will wither away and if we don't find a way to allow it to breathe within the safety of our garden, that plant will die off and very likely never have the strength it takes to grow healthily on its own.

If you are an anxious parent *the* best thing you can do for your child is to go on your own journey of healing from anxiety. Find a therapist. Get to the root of *why* it exists in the first place. Get on medication if you need to. Proactively begin taking care of *all* your self-care needs. Do it for your kids. Do it for you because you deserve that freedom.

 With love from a mom who totally gets it.
Naomi
xx

Social and Emotional Developmental Expectations According to Age

AGE	SOCIAL	EMOTIONAL
0-3		
3-6		
6-12		
13-18		

Stop worrying! If your child is cognitively and physically on track, and you're parenting for connection, they'll develop all the social and emotional skills when they are ready. Each flower blooms in its own time. Just keep watering and breathe.

The Importance of the 'Big Conversations' in Building Resilience

I got the 'sex talk' when I was about 12 years old. Actually, let me rephrase that – I never got the actual sex talk. My mom walked past my bedroom one day and popped a book about hamster babies on my bookshelf. That was it. Not a great foundation for a pretty significant topic!

Your kids and teens need to have the big conversations (the ones about child trafficking, drugs, LGBTQIA+, pornography, gender preferences, politics, wars) all the heavy, sometimes 'awkward' topics that they need to know about – from you.

As scary as it feels and as much as you may want to run in the opposite direction, your key to navigating these discussions successfully is to step into the heart of them without fear. When your child has questions, answer them honestly. For them to approach you with these mammoth topics in the first place you need to ensure that you have the kind of relationship with your child that feels safe to them – so ditch the judgement, the freak-out reactions, the 'never do that ...' or the opinions. You're going to need to appear unfazed and put on a face as though you're talking about what you're making for dinner.

Recently I had an 'all things drugs-related' conversation with my son over an early-morning round of the 'African' version of the game, Mancala. This was after we watched a young man, clearly high on drugs, walking up and down the beach and then casually sauntering on to our veranda. I explained and my son listened. He asked questions and I answered matter-of-factly and age-appropriately. That's all you need to do; our kids don't want the encyclopaedia version. You don't need to launch into excessive detail, just be relaxed and open enough so that your child feels safe to ask you anything.

What's important is that the first knowledge bank our children are creating on any of these big topics is from information and advice they receive from us, the people who they feel safest with and who are going to give them accurate information. We don't want them searching on Google or relying solely on peer input.

When we can honestly head into the heart of these issues with our children, they feel empowered and they won't get 'blown over' when they're confronted by these big life issues for the first time out there in the world. When they already have the knowledge from within the home, from you, it's just another brick in that foundation of their resilience building.

LET IT COME FROM YOU.

Childhood Depression and Resilience — Is That Even Possible?

I wish I didn't have to write a section on childhood depression, but it's a very real crisis that the world is facing and there has been a significant increase in the global prevalence of this mental-health burden over the past few years. While the words in this book have the potential to drastically change your relationship with your child (I have seen the impact in my own home and in the kids and teens I work with), it is essential to have a clear understanding of childhood depression and what it means.

Over my decades of psychotherapeutic work, I have worked with hundreds of depressed children and teens. I have also lived with one who has teetered on the edge of it. The year that it took to process and work through that darkness was the hardest year of my parenting life thus far.

I am so thankful that by holding the space every single day, by being the punchbag more often than not, by listening and hearing and then being able to make the situational changes that were needed, my child found new life and a new love for themselves, their school, their friends – everything that had for over 12 months hung like a dark cloud over the entire house.

Situational changes and holding spaces are not always going to be enough though. That's no one's fault and it certainly is *not* a reflection of your inability or a lack of care as a parent. The fact that you are reading this book is a powerful indication of exactly how much you *do* care and how much of a committed parent you *already* are.

When we realise that our children are struggling under the dark cloud of depression, it's easy to head down the vortex of self-blame. But judgement of ourselves and what we could have done or should have done are only going to lead to further disconnection between ourselves and our child.

A reminder to your parenting self: We always do the best we can with the physical and emotional resources we have and the knowledge that we have at the time. It is only when we know better that we can do better. Until then, leave guilt right outside the back door. This is not the time to be carrying this heavy emotional burden of responsibility – and one that is actually not yours to carry. During these times, more than ever, we need to compassionately embrace ourselves and our children.

While I do believe the words in this book hold some of the most important preventative steps for depression in our children and teens, depression may still be an extremely unwelcome guest knocking at your door. But with the foundation of resilience that you have been building as we have discussed here thus far and the self-work and reflection that you have been doing, it *is* possible for your children and teens to bounce out of the slump with less chance of being caught in the crossfire.

We do, however, need to be radically informed about this rapidly growing pandemic of mental-health challenges. We need to know the signs and what to do when we detect that our kids are struggling to break free of that dark cloud.

Most importantly, when you recognise any symptoms it is essential that you consult with a professional that you trust: your general practitioner, a paediatrician or paediatric specialist, a psychologist or child psychiatrist. Your child will need a great deal of support from a team-village (including family, friends, mental-health practitioners and medical experts) but healing *is* possible. Your medical practitioner may also prescribe medication for a period. There are many options available in this regard, but for the purposes of this book we are going to focus on the steps that you as parents can take.

RECOGNISING THE RED FLAGS

The earlier we recognise and act on these signs the better. Although it's normal for every single one of us to have 'off days' and 'bad patches', when these red flags last more than a few weeks and begin having an impact on family and peer relationships and academic work, then it's time to take action.

What is most important for parents to understand is that depression in children and teens can look like other things and can be the master of disguise. It may look like:

- Anger (Remember: that is just the outer 'onion' layer and often pain and sadness are some of the emotions that lie underneath)
- Disrespect (A child who has no respect for themself cannot respect anyone else)

- Social withdrawal (Things like no longer wanting to hang out with peers and preferring to be at home or in their bedroom)
- Being hyper-sensitive to criticism and rejection
- Frequent teary outbursts
- Ongoing psychosomatic complaints like headaches, stomach aches, etc.

And then the less-disguised symptoms such as:

- Trouble concentrating
- Fatigue and low energy
- Moodiness
- Changes in sleep and appetite
- Thoughts about dying and suicide.

A 10-STEP ACTION PLAN

1. Don't panic and incessantly question your child or teen. That will just lead to further disconnect and your *chief* priority here is connection. Do whatever you need to do to keep the gateway of communication open.

2. Make time in your schedule to 'hang out' with your child with zero expectations of what mood they should be in, what they should do or say, how grateful they should be feeling or what the outcome of the 'hang-out' should be. Watch a movie together, play a round of UNO, go out for lunch. Your child needs to be reminded that no matter how dark the cloud around their head is, you're not afraid of it and nothing makes them and their company

less lovable or worthy to you. Schedule family time and time with close friends. Although your child may not initially be leaping up and down at this idea, human-to-human connection is essential for healing.

3. Normalise depression and all other emotional spaces that are perfectly normal and 'human' to feel. Depression is not a 'sshhhh' word. A significant percentage of the population suffer from it so talk about it openly. Talk about how dark the world can feel when any of us are in that space. Let your child know the proactive steps that you are going to take to help them manage it and assure them of your presence as they navigate the journey.

4. Get into your child's world no matter how uncomfortable it is to be there. Remember, we don't have to fix things; we can't. Their best chance of walking through the fire and recognising that they are fireproof is knowing they have a parent who is willing to walk through it alongside them without trying to hose them down and yank them out. Your children need understanding and support no matter how dark the space is that they are in or how consuming the flames may feel.

5. Be patient. You are going to need this attribute in truckloads. Look after your *own* mental health first and that includes massive doses of self-care. As a psychologist-mom, I can tell you first hand that unless we are doing everything we can to regulate ourselves so that we are not triggered by our child's emotional space and behaviours, then inevitably we *react*, which often results in explosions and almost certainly in disconnection. When we are regulated we can take a step back, assess what our child actually needs and respond

to this. That's when deep connection takes place – when a human being in pain, of any age, feels heard.

6. Consult with a psychologist and set up a session for your child. It's important not to drill your child or teen after each session about what was said and to what degree they feel their depression has 'improved'. I know this is tough as it means relinquishing control to a space (a psychologist's office) that is not your own. For therapy of any sort to work, you need to trust the process. Don't request feedback from the psychologist after every session either. The healing of psychotherapy happens within the safety of the therapeutic space and the confidential relationship between your child and their therapist. Perhaps your part of this hard journey is learning to trust what you cannot control and that includes your child and their path. If there is a massive concern, your child's psychologist is ethically required to let you know about it. If you keep building a strong connection with your child and don't invasively ask about how therapy went, but rather focus on the 'hanging out' part, they will tell you all that they want to in their own way and in their own time.

7. You may need to consult with a psychiatrist to assess your child for medication. There is *nothing* wrong with your child if they need to be on medication. We wouldn't deprive a child with pneumonia from taking antibiotics and we need to get rid of all the mental-health stigmas that might exist in our own minds surrounding depression, anxiety and medication to manage anything related to mental health. If your child's psychologist and psychiatrist feel that medication is warranted,

trust them and trust your child. Your child will be able to let you know whether the medication prescribed is having the desired result. The psychiatrist or your chosen medical practitioner will inform you about any side effects that you need to be aware of. I see too many people (teens and adults) who only take medication to address mental-health diagnoses, whereas it's essential that psychotherapy and lifestyle changes are also prioritised. When we treat depression or anxiety solely with medication, it's like pouring water on a raging fire. The water may contain the fire for a while, but ultimately, to extinguish the fire, we need to get to the source of what's causing its ignition in the first place. We cannot neglect making holistic changes if we really want to put out the fire of depression.

8. Seek your own support during this challenging time. I highly recommend talking to your own therapist. Navigating the journey with a depressed child or teen has an impact on all family members. You'll be taking a lot of punches for a lot of reasons, and for your sake *and* your family's sake, find a safe space of your own.

9. Don't forget to have fun. Yes – you, the parent. This is an essential and overlooked part of soul-filling. Go out for coffee with a friend, take surfing lessons, head to book club (or wine club or whatever your version is called), play Twister in the lounge. Laugh. Let go. Be in that moment of joy. Dark skies find it much easier to hold storm clouds so lighten yours in whatever way you can.

10. Most importantly, just be there. Keep holding on. When the storm is over, what's most important is that your child knew exactly where you were standing while it raged. As much as you feel pushed away some days, your

place through the turbulence should be right by
their side.

While depression is a serious illness, it's important to remember
that it's very treatable and the right interventions make all the
difference. You are reading this so your path to a different ending
has already begun.

'YOU SAY YOU'RE "DEPRESSED". ALL
I SEE IS RESILIENCE. YOU ARE
ALLOWED TO FEEL MESSED UP
AND INSIDE OUT. IT DOESN'T MEAN
YOU'RE DEFECTIVE. IT
JUST MEANS YOU'RE HUMAN.'

David Mitchell

The Highly Sensitive Child (HSC) and Resilience

Highly sensitive children (HSC) are exceptional human beings. At first, the words 'sensitive' and 'resilient' might not seem like they can co-occur, but they most certainly can.

WHAT DOES AN HSC LOOK LIKE?

You might be experiencing some or all of the below in your home:

- Sunshine OR thunder (normal light-grey skies don't often exist)
- A black-and-white thinker (any tiptoeing into grey means a meltdown)
- A strong sense of justice and a very switched-on moral compass (becoming highly upset when any wrong is done to self or others)

- Extremely sensitive and easily overwhelmed by sensory stimuli – smells, sounds, touch, visuals
- The impact of too little sleep, no food, unhealthy food and illness seems about 100 times as strong as the impact on other children
- Lower levels of frustration tolerance (not great in sibling-rivalry situations)
- Seemingly non-compliant and very strong-willed personality (reframe: leaders in the making)
- Very perceptive to and impacted on by other people's emotions
- Sensitivity to pain (even greater physical reactions to things like stings, bites, rashes etc.)
- High levels of empathy
- Sensitive to changes in daily routine
- Needs a great deal of alone time in between socialising to feel regulated again.

In my practice and in my home, I have ongoing, first-hand experience with all of the above almost every single day. Because an HSC's nervous system is easily dysregulated, they feel emotionally and physically overwhelmed more easily than a child who doesn't possess the gift of high sensitivity.

In my experience, our HSC are the ones our world needs so many more of. They see an injustice, feel devastated by it and then throw themselves into action to stand up for the underdog and do something about it. These potential future world changers also have the capacity to be extremely resilient. Here are some things to consider that will help them become exactly that:

🦋 Most importantly, from the youngest age, reframe their sensitivity as being a gift. They're going to hear words like, 'Stop being so sensitive' often over their lifetime, but don't let them hear those words, or anything that remotely resembles them, coming out of your mouth. I'm not going to try to sugar-coat sensitivity; as a sensitive person myself and a mom of two sensitive beings (one the epitome of an HSC), sensitivity is certainly *not* without its burdens. An HSC's ability to feel the world more deeply also enables them to recognise the beauty in the small things that much more easily. That's a tick in the resilience box – the ability to pause and notice and to be fully appreciative of the people and natural world around us.

🦋 You're going to need to hold the space SO much. You're going to need to do your own breathing and own regulating a whole lot more often too. Because the HSC's brain is more easily dysregulated, *your* ability to co-regulate with them in times of overwhelm is essential because, remember, the brain wiring for regulation can only develop when an uncalm brain is in the presence of a calm and regulated one.

🦋 And this is the last time, I promise. Remember that it's not personal. Once you have calmed yourself right down, head back to the 'lighthouse questions' of 'What does my child need right now?' and 'How can I be kind and present in this moment?'

On the days you want to scream, break down or run away, try to remind yourself that your calm presence is changing your child's neurological wiring. You are going to see the incredible impact of all the 'space holding' that you do (maybe not for a few years, but you *will* see it).

Our highly sensitive children feel more and, because of that, parenting *is* harder. Let the fact that they feel things so deeply remind you that what drives you up the wall some days is exactly what places your child in so much more of a position to be a world healer.

Helping the Grieving
Child and Teen

A considerable percentage of my practice is helping children, teens and adults deal with grief. The grieving process for children and teens is very different to adults. It is so important for us to understand these differences so that the various stages of grief can be processed safely. If for any reason this cannot (or does not) happen, it can become a playground for the development of anxiety and depression that ultimately extends well into adulthood.

In order to fully support children and teens through the process of loss and help them heal, it is essential that we understand HOW they grieve, and that we know what to expect on their journey.

Grief can be experienced as a result of *any* loss in life and presents itself in a variety of contexts: the loss of loved ones, pets, homes, friendships – any relationship – or even objects that have played a significant role (gifts, heirlooms etc.) in the life of a child.

In this section, however, I am going to focus primarily on the loss of human loved ones.

Side note: As adults we underestimate how important pets are for our children.

For some, pets are their best friends, the ones they go home to, cry with, play with. They are family members and children may (intensely) grieve for them for a long period of time. I see many children and teens in my practice who talk lovingly about the animals they lost many years earlier. My son still tells me how much he misses his chicken who died well over a year ago. This feathered being had definitely been one of his best friends and my son's sense of loss was profound.

Grief is a normal emotion that we expect after the death of a loved one. The closer the relationship, the deeper the intensity of the loss the child and teen will experience.

THE ROLLER COASTER OF GRIEF

Children grieve and display their emotions differently to adults. It's easy to underestimate a child's grief because of this difference, but it is vital to remember that they don't grieve 'less' than adults and their pain is no easier.

While teens are likely to experience the weight of grief similarly to adults, children 'dip' into grief. From an adult's perspective, they seem to oscillate between seeming to be okay (playing, laughing, interacting with friends), dipping back into the 'heavier' morose emotions and then cycling back to seeming 'fine'. And so this continues on loop – it's a roller coaster for them.

As adults we might find that confusing – perhaps even frustrating – or assume that the loss hasn't really impacted on them. This is a normal way for children to grieve.

COMMON EMOTIONS OF GRIEF

Everybody's grief journey is different. There is no right or wrong way to grieve. You may only see a few of the common emotions and some children (and adults) may not experience all of them. Here are some of the familiar ones:

⑩ Denial and shock

These are often the first ones that surface after a significant loss. As with any behaviour that a child displays or words they use, there's always a message. Young children may think that the person has temporarily 'gone away'. Some children may say, 'My daddy's on holiday' or 'My dad's gone on a business trip.' This is because the reality of the loss is far more than the child can process, both emotionally and developmentally. This is normal and our role as adults is NOT to correct them with 'cold facts' by saying things like, 'No, that's not true. Your father's dead.' We need to be patient, support them and reflect what they're really feeling. Our response to their emotional space is to understand their pain and confusion. When a child is in a state of denial and says something like, 'My daddy's on holiday' meet them at their level, make eye contact and gently reflect, 'You really miss your dad and you wish he was here.' There's no need to say more than that.

Our job is to understand that message and reflect it in order for our children to feel safe enough to process their grief.

⑩ Guilt and frustration

These are two big emotions that go hand in hand with grief. Guilt is a feeling that we don't often think about. From our adult perspective, it can be hard to understand why our children and teens may feel guilty when they've had nothing to do with the death of a loved one. Guilt shows up in many forms and for so many reasons and it is a very contaminating emotion that hinders our path to healing along the grief journey. I work with lots of children, teens and young adults who feel guilty because they didn't say 'goodbye' during the last interaction they had with the loved one. Naturally, the 'if only' thoughts stem from that guilt. 'If only I had done this, said that, been there ...'

Young children, depending on their age, may attribute a death to something that they said or did even though the two events are clearly unrelated from our adult perspectives. For example, a child may think, 'If only I hadn't misbehaved the day before', 'If only I hadn't been cross with Daddy', 'If only I had told Mom I loved her when she said it to me', 'If only (complete with an endless amount of options), then Mommy wouldn't have died'.

Be very aware of guilt and the heaviness it brings. The best way to work through guilt is to create a safe space where children can talk about ALL their emotions. When a child has space to share their vulnerability, overwhelm and sadness with us, and we reflect and normalise the emotions, it enables them to process their grief.

⓪ Anger

Anger is an exceptionally common emotion along the journey of grief. Your child or teen may be angry with you, the deceased person, or even with God. It's essential to remember that at the core of anger is disempowerment. Anger is never *just* anger. It is the externalisation of sadness, a defence against pain, hurt and vulnerability. It requires patience, compassion and understanding in order for it to find its release.

⓪ Anxiety

Anyone who has lost someone that they love will know that their entire world changes and it will never be the same again. There's often an underlying fear of the unknown – a completely new and unwanted future. This space naturally creates a foundation of anxiety.

While a child is re-navigating their 'new world', it is not

uncommon to see an increase in generalised anxiety, separation anxiety and children who fear being alone. Some children may even feel abandoned by their loved one who has departed. These are all very normal emotional spaces.

⑪ Depression

Depression – especially in situations when a child has not been able to process their grief – commonly occurs as a result of losing a significant person. (See the section 'Childhood Depression and Resilience – Is That Even Possible?') When I lost my mom to cancer during my teen years, I fell into a deep state of depression. Looking back, I realise how much of that was because I wasn't allowed to grieve. I was expected to move on and accept her death as 'The will of God'. As a result of my pain not being heard and normalised, I landed in the depths of despair and it took me years to recover from it.

Grief cannot be rushed. It must be 'sat in' and waded through for as long as necessary, in an environment where children do not feel judged for any of the emotions they may be feeling. Children need your unconditional support and patience in order to be able to do this.

Remember: There's no limit as to what emotions the grief process may hold or how long they can be felt for.

PHYSICAL SYMPTOMS AND COMMON BEHAVIOURS ASSOCIATED WITH GRIEF

When children and teens find it difficult to verbalise what they are feeling, they may show physical symptoms of grief. Some of these may include:

- Tummy aches
- Headaches
- Body pains.

Behavioural changes are also common following the death of a loved one. Here are a few examples:

◀ Sleep difficulties

At the beginning of the grief journey the world feels unsafe for children and teens. Younger children may need you to stay with them while they fall asleep. They may need a comfort object – an item that belongs to you or the deceased. They may also want to sleep in your bedroom for a while.

◀ Developmental regression

Developmental regression occurs when a child seems to lose previously acquired skills. It is not uncommon in younger children experiencing grief.

For example, a child who may have been potty-trained suddenly starts bedwetting or messing in their pants, or they might need comfort toys even though these have been packed away in the cupboard for years. Your child may start sucking their thumb or two fingers, throwing tantrums and having meltdowns.

Remember: Regression happens any time when a child doesn't feel safe and secure. This regression is not permanent. As soon as their world begins to settle again, which may take a while, you'll see them easing out of the regression.

TAKING ON ADULT RESPONSIBILITIES

Often, particularly the oldest child (or the only child), takes on adult responsibilities after the death of a parent in order to ease the load for the surviving parent. Sometimes it's as a result of hearing a well-meaning adult pass a comment such as, 'You are the man of the house now' or 'Take care of your siblings.' These types of comments place considerable pressure on any child and teen and significantly increase the level of anxiety. Healing will not happen when children feel that they need to be adults. Healing can only happen when they are allowed to process their grief feeling like they have a trusted adult to help them do this.

THE IMPORTANCE OF PLAY IN GRIEF

When a child is grieving, you are likely to see changes in the way they play and the type of play they engage in. They may suddenly prefer to play by themselves, or perhaps a child who has always enjoyed their own company may suddenly need you or a playmate. Bear in mind that play is extremely important in all aspects of development for our children.

Our children process their world around them through play and this includes how they work through trauma and loss. Play is an essential part of healing so encourage it. Let them play freely and make it part of their world. Be mindful of the 'over-busy', overscheduled world we so often live in. Wherever possible, make sure there's time for play as this is where they'll experience the most powerful healing.

CHANGES IN SCHOOL FUNCTIONING

The grieving child or teen may start showing a number of school-related difficulties. Frequently, children struggle with concentration and focus. When we grieve, we experience many overwhelming emotions. Big emotions stem from our limbic system, but the part of our brain we use for learning and concentration is our prefrontal cortex. When the two are in competition, the limbic system always wins. This means that your child will most likely be unable to focus properly at school – either for a short while or it may go on for an extended period of time. They may struggle to pay attention and finish their tasks or activities.

On the other hand, you may also see an increase in academic achievement in children who are grieving. In order to ward off depression or anxiety, or in an attempt to please a deceased parent, a child may compensate and work even harder. They'll place an incredible amount of pressure on themselves to 'perform'. Be aware that you may see either side of that spectrum and both of these are signs that our children are struggling.

GRIEF THROUGH THE AGES

Children are never too young to grieve. I often hear parents say, 'They were too young to remember' or 'They were too young to have been impacted on.' Children of all ages are impacted upon by the loss of a significant person in their lives. Although there is no 'one-size-fits-all', the list below highlights some of the differences you may expect to see from a developmental perspective.

Babies (0–2 years):
- Children of this age have no understanding of the concept of death.
- They are aware of the separation from the deceased loved one.
- They may react with increased crying, decreased responsiveness and changes in their eating and/or sleeping habits.
- They may keep looking/asking for a deceased family member.

The biggest aspect impacting children of this age is the emotional state of the surviving family members.

Early years (3–6 years):
- Children of this age are curious about death but believe it is temporary and reversible.
- They do not understand the permanence of death. They are present-orientated.
- They may see the deceased as being dead, but believe that they are still capable of limited functions (e.g. that they will keep breathing/eating after death).
- They may see the deceased as someone who is sleeping.
- They will often feel guilty as if they did something that resulted in the person 'going away'.
- They may think they can make the deceased person come back to life with good behaviour.
- Children often worry about who will take care of them. They are concerned about being left behind and being alone.
- They are very impacted upon by the emotional space of family members.
- Children may struggle to express their emotions verbally. They express themselves behaviourally through acting out, showing physical symptoms, having sleeping difficulties and demonstrating regression in their development.
- They may ask the same questions repeatedly.
- This age group tends to need a great deal of reassurance.
- Play is extremely important for all ages, but especially at this stage. Play is a healing outlet for grief.

Primary-school children (6–12 years):
- The thought process of the child at this age surrounding death has matured.
- They may initially want to see death as reversible, but at around six or seven years of age they begin to understand the finality of death.
- They may think of and refer to the deceased as an angel, spirit, skeleton or ghost.
- Children of this age require more details of the death and show more interest in specific details such as what happens to the body after death.
- They have more concern for how others around them are dealing with death.
- By the age of ten, children understand that death happens to everyone and cannot be avoided.
- They may experience a range of emotions, including guilt, anger, shame, anxiety and/or sadness.
- They often begin to worry about their own death and may become overly fearful of their own sickness and injury.
- They may struggle to verbalise emotions and will demonstrate how they are feeling through behaviours such as school avoidance, aggression, physical symptoms and withdrawal from family and friends.
- Children may present with clinginess to caregivers.
- They may feel insecure and abandoned and worry about who will take care of them if their caregivers die.
- They may attribute blame to themselves for contributing in some way towards the death of a loved one.

Teens (13–18 years):
- Teens have an adult understanding of the concept of death, but often do not have an adult's experience and coping mechanisms.
- They may act out in anger at family members or show reckless, impulsive behaviours.
- There may be an increase in behaviours such as conflict with peers and siblings, substance abuse or sexual promiscuity.
- Teens are likely to experience a wide range of emotions, but struggle to deal with them and often feel uncomfortable chatting about them.
- They tend to question their faith and grapple with an understanding of the world.
- They may not be receptive to support from family members and may need to feel separate and independent during their grieving journey.
- They may want to spend more time in the company of friends and peers as a coping strategy.
- Teens may become more withdrawn and want to be alone.
- They will need to be encouraged to talk or seek external support. If they do not want to receive support from caregivers for any reason they should be encouraged to engage with a close teacher or therapist.

THE MOST IMPORTANT PART OF HELPING A GRIEVING CHILD

The most important ingredient in supporting our children through grief is the same as with any aspect of parenting and educating – it's ourselves. *We* have to process the loss of our loved ones and go on that journey of healing because *we* are our children's role models. Children draw strength from the adults in their lives.

Your children will learn how to process their grief through the way you process yours. If you sweep it under the proverbial carpet, they're going to feel as if their huge emotions are illegitimate, unjustified and abnormal. Never rob them of such an important part of healing. Being able to normalise emotions, process them, own them, and acknowledge them is THE most important step forward in working through grief.

While it's important to share our emotions with our children, we need to be hyper-aware of not burdening them otherwise our emotions become our children's deep grief to carry.

If you want to help your child, find a counsellor, a grief therapist or psychologist to support *you*. It's the greatest gift that you can give them and the most powerful way to help them. Children need to be able to focus on their healing without worrying about and carrying the weight of your emotions. What our children need most is our own healing. If our children feel that we cannot process our grief, or that we are struggling, they will most likely hide their own emotions.

THE IMPORTANCE OF NORMALISING EMOTIONS

I can't emphasise this enough – NORMALISE the emotions surrounding grief. In all aspects and areas, no matter what the emotion is. These can feel huge and overwhelming, but become so much more manageable when we know we are not alone and that emotions such as guilt or frustration are a normal part of the grieving experience.

When I'm working with kids and I pull out my EmotionOcean

cards (the link can be found in the Resources section at the back of this book) and I talk about how normal it is to feel grief, anger and all these uncomfortable and hard emotions, they are relieved to know that universally they're not the only ones that feel this. This also enables them to understand that there is no right or wrong way to grieve and there's no set of emotions that we should or shouldn't feel. In times of grief, trauma and any disempowerment it's small things such as normalising emotions that help empower a child and help them realise that they are not alone. When we dismiss emotions our children are left feeling as if there's something wrong with them.

Make it a habit of talking about feelings in your home, whether it's grief-related or not. So many of the depressed teens and young adults who I see in therapy have been raised in homes where emotions are left unaddressed. This often happens because it's too difficult for the adults to stay in these big, messy emotional spaces, but if we don't talk about these overwhelming and uncomfortable emotions, our children become burdened with them.

Expect these big emotions along the grief journey so that when they arrive you can hold the space for them.

One of the simplest quotes on the importance of emotions is also one of the most powerful.

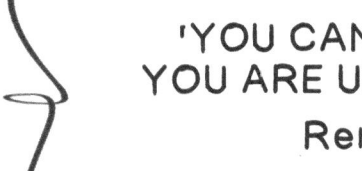

'YOU CANNOT HEAL WHAT YOU ARE UNWILLING TO FEEL.'
Renée Fishman

GRIEF CAN'T BE 'FIXED'

We can't 'fix' our children's pain. We can't make it disappear with an ice cream, the latest computer game, a smart watch or whatever else we think may bring temporary relief. We need to face the hard reality alongside them – nothing we do can fix or bring back the loved ones we have lost. What our children need most from us is to hold the space and grieve alongside them without overwhelming them with our emotional space.

We would never intend for our burdens or emotional space to become our child's responsibility, but without a strong support network of our own this can happen very easily. This can manifest as anxiety and depression in our children. It is essential at this time to lean on your friends and your own circle of support to help you process your grief and walk your healing journey.

BELIEFS ABOUT THE AFTERLIFE

Whatever beliefs you have about the afterlife, share them with your child. Children find it comforting to know that, in whatever form, the deceased lives on in some way. Talk about this often and talk about the lost loved one, wherever you believe their spirit lives on.

Death isn't an end; it is a part of everyone's story and life process. In terms of helping them cope, and from research done on resilience, having some kind of understanding about an afterlife helps significantly. Perhaps for your family this is nature, heaven, the stars. Whatever it may be, share it with them. Talk about the journey, the story of death, of loss and of grief. Life and loss are threads woven into each of our journeys.

WITHHOLD ALL JUDGEMENT AND KEEP TALKING

Don't judge your children's emotions no matter what they are. Just be there to hold the space. They're allowed to be angry with God. They're allowed to be angry with you. They're allowed to experience any of these huge, overwhelming emotions. Just hold the space. Talk about the deceased loved one. A significant hindrance in the grief process is when adults in a home simply stop talking about someone who has died because of the emotions it brings up within them. Sometimes they even take down all the photographs because the constant visual reminder of the loss brings so much pain. But removing reminders of loved ones can make the grieving process that much harder for our children. They need the photos – we all do. They need to keep talking about the loved one because talking about someone keeps their memory alive. It communicates the message that the person still matters, that they still exist in our hearts and minds and that we are still allowed to remember and grieve the void that they have left.

If your beliefs allow, put up photos of your lost loved one around the house and let your child choose photos to put up in their bedroom.

 REMINDER: Grief is disempowering. Any choice that your child or teen can make, however small it may seem, is empowering.

Keep the loved one alive by making them a part of your conversations. Talk about their favourite food, their favourite flavour of ice cream, the funny things that you used to do, the laughs you had about the Netflix series you watched together, the games that you used to play in the garden, the things that frustrated you. Talk about the hard things. Remember that these things may bring the tears, and may bring fresh pain, but they're so important to help us keep the memory of them alive and to acknowledge that although the person may be gone physically, they are alive and present in our memories.

BOUNDARIES AND ROUTINES PROVIDE STABILITY IN THE 'UPSIDE DOWN'

Boundaries and routines are so important, yet often in times of trauma and loss these are the things that go out the window first. While it's normal during times of shock and immediately following a death for things to be a little upside down in a household, it is critical to remember that the stormier and more unpredictable the sea, the more calm we need from the 'normal everyday' things. People bring meals. Bedtime is later. Boundaries and routines are an essential part of our children's sense of safety and security.

We need to be consistent and remember them as important pillars in the home. While our expectations of our children need to change during times of loss and trauma, through gentle parenting, compassion, understanding and patience, we need to implement the 'usual' boundaries as lovingly as possible. The message we give our children in doing that is: 'Your world may have been turned upside down, but in this house you are safe and the way we do things in this home (as far as possible) stays the same'.

THE IMPORTANCE OF QUIET

There is a temptation to get back to work, to get back to life, to get back to the rush of how things used to be in the aftermath of losing a loved one. We often do this in an attempt to ward off uncomfortable feelings of loss and pain. It is important that our children feel that we are not pushing the grief away and forgetting. Life does need to carry on, but we need to make sure that we're spending time to check in, to spend quieter family time and to spend one-on-one time with our children.

It's in these quieter times that children feel safe and can allow themselves to feel vulnerable enough to be able to express their emotions and all that they are feeling without judgement.

GRIEF WILL RESURFACE

After the initial symptoms of grief have eased, there is likely to be a period of time when your child seems to be coping better. For many children, grief will resurface again at new developmental stages (adolescence, adulthood etc.) or on occasions such as high-school dances, passing their driving test, the first day of school, or a wedding day. During any big life events, your child may feel the loss more acutely, even if it happened decades earlier. At these times it's worthwhile remembering what grief looks like and offering support to your child (even your adult child) through them. These may also be the times when your child will benefit from a 'check-in' with a psychologist or grief counsellor.

DOES MY CHILD NEED THERAPY?

Many children and teens benefit from therapy to help them through the grieving process. Once this relationship has been established, it's common for them to need to dip back into therapy every now and then to touch base for one or two sessions, just to help them process all they are re-experiencing.

There are times when it is essential to get your child and teen the support they need as soon as possible. Look out for any of the signs below:

- Your child has been experiencing symptoms of grief for six months or longer
- They're having repeated nightmares
- You see them displaying or participating in any self-harming behaviour
- They are experiencing suicidal ideation and repeatedly state, for example, that they want to be with the deceased
- You see grief symptoms worsen with time and your child seems to be in an extended period of depression
- There is the ongoing belief that the world is unsafe
- You notice ongoing behaviour problems that do not seem to ease, despite the length of time or the amount of processing or support that you're giving them
- They are excessively imitating or talking to the deceased person
- Extended withdrawal from family and friends and wanting to be alone all the time
- Ongoing and complete denial that the person is deceased
- There's no expression of emotion.

These are all urgent cries for help and need immediate intervention from medical and mental-health professionals who are experienced in grief work.

HOW CAN EDUCATORS HELP?

During times of grief, educators are in one of the most important positions to be able to help children simply because of the amount of time and the degree of interaction that they have with them on a daily basis. It's important for them to be knowledgeable about and aware of signs that a child is just not coping. They need to be flexible with the expectations of the child to study for tests and exams, complete all their homework or even sit still through an entire lesson.

Grieving children may need to be allowed to take a walk in the school gardens. They may need some time to go and chat to a trusted adult, to have a good cry somewhere. (In my experience, compassionate media-centre educators are often trusted 'go-to' people.) These kinds of 'breathing spaces' are important to identify with a child; it helps so much for them to know they have a safe support person on the school premises who they can check in with.

Come up with a signal that a child can give you that communicates they need time out so that they don't need to ask your permission each time. As it is for the home environment, it's essential that the classroom becomes a place where emotions are normalised and that the grief process is spoken about. Classrooms should be spaces that focus on the development of emotional literacy, empathy and kindness. Children should know that it's absolutely okay to feel happy and be playing in a fantasy world with their friends one minute and want to sit in the corner of the classroom and cry the next. If you are an educator and have a grieving child in your classroom, try and check in with them and spend a little extra time with them in some way. If it's a teen, it may just mean playing a three-minute round of UNO with them a few times a week. The message you want to communicate is: 'I am here if you need me.'

HOW CAN WE HELP OUR CHILDREN TO REMEMBER AND TO PROCESS THEIR LOSS?

There are so many ways to do this, but here are a few ideas:

- ✓ MEMORY BOXES: I often make memory boxes with the children I work with or I encourage families to make them together. Get a sturdy box of any shape or size and let your child decorate it however they want. It is like a treasure box; they can put letters in the box, they can choose small items of the deceased person, they can put in photographs or just about anything that helps them remember the loved one and is significant to them in any way. Maybe they want to write a letter to their lost family member or maybe they want to draw a picture. Let THEM decide (remember: it is all about empowerment). It's their box to add their special memories. Once created, the box can be stored in their cupboard, under their bed, in the lounge or anywhere they can access it whenever they want to.

When my mom died many, many years ago, I had a box and in it I kept all the letters she wrote to me while I was at university. I kept photos; I kept the little funeral pamphlet and letters that others had written to me about the impact she had on their lives. I still have it to this day and every so often, over the almost three decades since she died, I have taken it out, gone through it, remembered and cried. It's a release. Memory boxes can be a wonderful way for our children to keep feeling connected to the special person they have lost.

- ✓ PHOTO BOOKS: There are so many wonderful apps you can use to make photo books. Insert little write-ups of memories, photos and really anything you want in it. This could be a project that your child or teen does on their own or it could be something you do together. Get it printed into a coffee-table book or a special book that can be kept on your child's bookshelf or somewhere else in your home.

✔ PHOTOS: Depending on your religion, and if it's allowed, put up photos of the deceased person around the house or add to those already in the home. Your children need to know that you are not trying to create a new life by erasing memories. Let your child choose a few to print out and take them frame shopping. Let them decide where in the house or their bedroom they want to hang the photos.

✔ JOURNAL WRITING: Journal writing is a powerful healer in the grieving process. It is something that I recommend and see tremendous benefits in my patients of all ages. If your child is old enough, encourage them to write a journal. Allowing them to choose a journal and buying them new stationery are great ways to begin this process.

✔ PROJECT CREATION: So many of the children I work with express their emotions and process their grief through projects that involve creation. It's empowering to be able to create. Creations can be in multiple forms, ranging from drawing pictures to mosaic-making, clay work, making bracelets or necklaces and doing beadwork — where each bead signifies something that they remember about the person — or even planting a tree or a garden that holds significance and memories for the child or teen. There's no limit to how many ways grief can be expressed. Discuss ideas with them and follow your child's lead in how they want to express their loss. I have known parents who have had teddy bears made for their children out of fabric from a deceased parent's pyjamas. I love this idea and these teddy bears have become children's most treasured possessions.

THE TOUGH FIRSTS

It's easy to forget that the firsts are often the hardest; the first birthday without the deceased, theirs and the child's, the first Christmas, the first Mother's/Father's Day, the first anniversary of their death, the first family holiday, the first New Year – all the firsts are hard. As educators, as parents, as any caregiver in a child's life, don't ignore these firsts or gloss over them hoping the day just goes by. They need to be acknowledged and on these occasions it brings comfort to remember the deceased in some way. I still, more than 25 years later, buy a bunch of red roses on the anniversary of my mom's death and on her birthday. It's my little thing between me and her and it's my way of saying, 'Hey, Mom, I still miss you and you are still a part of my life.'

It helps to remember that any happy occasion and celebration is likely going to have a little twinge of grief and pain associated with it because our loved one is not there to celebrate it with us. Acknowledge the sadness and honour the person in some way on these occasions.

THE WORDS WE SAY

It's human nature to make statements like, 'It will be okay. Time will heal.' When it comes to grief, time alone doesn't heal. We need to refrain from saying these words. We don't ever heal and fill the void completely. Time doesn't make it okay, but we learn to cope with the grief. We learn to grow with it on a completely new journey.

The words we say in an attempt to offer condolences often mean nothing and they can even create anger and resentment, especially when a child or a teen is really battling to cope. The most powerful words at this time remain, and will always be, 'I AM HERE.' Sometimes no words are needed; just be there and be near in silence.

FINAL CONSIDERATIONS

Don't try to fix a grieving person. You can't. Don't try to sweep your grief or your child's away. You can't. If you try to just 'move on' you're going to end up making your child feel that there is something wrong with them, and they're going to be completely overwhelmed by those big emotions that they feel.

Sit in those big, overwhelming emotions with them without fearing them. Just hold the space for the raging storms as your children grieve and remember, you're allowed to grieve alongside them. Get your own support for your grief journey so that your emotional space doesn't become a burden for your child. You cannot hold the emotional space for your child unless you are looking after your own. Our children will not open up to us about their emotional space unless they feel that we are coping with ours or that we have put steps in place to help ourselves during this time. Normalise all of their feelings, share the memories and create an emotional space where your child feels that they can share and talk about their loved one without upsetting you.

After the initial grieving period, you will need to reconstruct the family unit through a journey that is going to be painful. Healing through pain happens through connection, through being together, through building relationships, through that one-on-one time, through those family moments of having fun together, of crying together, of creating new family traditions. Bond, play board games, watch movies – whatever you do, just hang out together. Doing all this is hard and it is sore, but it is important and it is healing.

Grief is a journey and it's essential to find ways to have happiness in the moment and create memories that are filled with love and laughter through it. Patience and compassion are two of the most important things you're going to need. You're likely going to have to answer a lot of questions. Your children are likely to fall apart, as you are, and they're likely to fall apart again. Grief isn't something we move beyond; we grow around it.

The grief journey is like a maze. It's going to take a long time to navigate your way through it. Some days we hit a wall. Some days we stumble backwards. Some days we take the wrong path. Some days we step in the wrong direction. Some days we have to start all over again, but the most important thing is that every day we keep moving. Healing for us as humans, for our children, for ourselves, comes from knowing that we are not alone.

Normalise it. Walk your own path. Be there to hold the space and please reach out to a professional if you need to.

Tips for Parents Who are Divorced

Over the years, I've worked with hundreds of couples who are divorced (or are divorcing) and their children. Of all these, only TWO couples were ever able to work together and co-parent amicably in their children's best interests. Only TWO. Too often, because of the anger and hurt parents feel towards the other, children become the victims.

Divorce is undeniably challenging for kids of all ages, but there is so much that parents can do to ensure that their children thrive regardless of the trying situation they find themselves in. Your children, like you, will go through an adjustment period in which overwhelming emotions and certain behaviours are common. These may include:

◀ Anxiety

◀ Stress

◀ Clinginess

- ◁ Moodiness
- ◁ Regression
- ◁ Difficulty concentrating
- ◁ Changes in school marks
- ◁ Withdrawal
- ◁ Appetite changes – bingeing, refusing to eat and/or disliking foods they usually eat.

Anything goes and these are all just signs of your child understandably feeling disempowered. If you've made the difficult decision to separate, here are some important guidelines to remember:

- ⑪ The question that should always be at the forefront of your mind, as well as your decisions, should be 'Is this in my child's best interests?' Too often our actions and words are intended as a reaction to the other parent, yet they are extremely hurtful to our children and ultimately damage our relationship with them.

- ⑪ Children are far more likely to thrive in two 'calmer' homes as opposed to one in which there's instability, hostility and conflict. It's important to remember that your children learn how to manage their future relationships by observing you. Staying together 'for the sake of the children' often results in a toxic home environment that only leads to mental-health difficulties for every family member – with the greatest impact, naturally, being on the children.

- ⑪ The greater the hostility between parents during the period of divorce and/or separation, the greater the negative impact on the child(ren). The longer the custody battle and 'war' continues, the greater the child suffers. Few battles are carried out with the child's best interests at heart. It's worthwhile remembering this through the legal process.

ⓜ It goes without saying that your instinct is to rush to help your kids, but please – go on your own journey first. The more healed you are, the more you are going to be able to show up and be the parent your child needs during a time in their life when their world as they have always known it is being tipped on its head. If you are locked in depression, sadness, anger and hurt, you won't be able to show up for your child.

ⓜ Get your kids into counselling where they'll have a neutral space to talk confidentially about how they are *really* feeling. Too often in divorce situations kids are left in the middle of two warring parents. Because children fear upsetting either one or both parents, they'll keep their emotions guarded. This closed-up state will only lead to depression and anxiety. Find your children an objective space and don't badger the therapist for information on the session or the other parent. Trust this space so that it can be one of safety and healing for your child.

ⓜ Do everything you can to communicate amicably with your ex-partner. Remember, your children are sponges and they absorb everything. Your annoyed sighs and sideline comments about their other parent will not go unnoticed. Every time you say anything that puts the other parent down, it's an emotional burden for your children to carry.

ⓜ It's common for one of the parents to feel guilt; for asking for the divorce or initiating the break-up, feeling like they have irreparably damaged their children and feeling like they don't spend enough time with them. Guilt contaminates parenting. It often leads to changing or altering boundaries (essential for feeling grounded during times of instability), trying to 'make up' for the hurt and less time by over-compensating (excessive giving or saying 'yes' to everything). Children don't feel safe with the parent who's doing all the 'spoiling'. They feel safe with the parent who is consistent, holds the boundaries and sticks to routine ... surprise, surprise!

ⓜ Normalise all emotions. Allow your child to feel anger, sadness, overwhelm and whatever else may come their way. Guilt is also a common emotion for children to experience in a separation. What matters most is to talk openly about the varying emotions as and when needed, and be very aware not to punish the behaviour that stems from the emotional space they're in.

ⓜ It is imperative not to take your child's emotional space personally. Children will act out, overreact, say hurtful things, and behave in ways that you may feel are an attack on you. It's easier said than done, but remember that it is not personal and the best you can do is not react to any of it. They're just communicating to you how disempowered they feel in a world where a major decision relating to their family unit is out of their control.

ⓜ Be honest and age-appropriate when speaking to your child about the divorce or separation. This does not mean putting the blame on the other parent and disclosing all the 'wrongs' done in your marriage or relationship. Ideally, what you communicate should be that not all problems in adult relationships can be resolved and sometimes parents decide that they will be happier without one another. Your children need to know that the divorce is not their fault and was not because of anything they said or did. Stick to simple facts and, as tempting as it may be, avoid blame and judgement at all costs. The only ones who suffer when adults offload their opinions are the children whose shoulders they land on. Don't give your children hope that you will get back together. They'll be looking for this and it will only create more devastation if they have any unrealistic expectations.

⑩ Children cope far better emotionally when they're able to have healthy relationships with both parents. While it is a parent's responsibility to ensure that their relationship with their child is a strong one, be aware of not doing or saying anything to your child that may become an obstacle in the way of a healthy bond with both of you.

CLOSING THOUGHTS

Adjusting to a new normal can take time. Be patient, and most importantly, take yourself on a healing journey. Whether we are divorced, separated or still in an intact family unit, our own healing remains our number-one priority when raising emotionally healthy and secure children.

Boundaries and Discipline — The 'How-To' Guide

In my home we follow a values-based approach to give us all the guidelines as to how we need to work together as a family – as a team. It may be that you are wanting more in terms of how to manage behaviours that require limits and how to gently and compassionately put boundaries in place. This is an issue requiring a book of its own, but I've tried to summarise what I believe are the most important reminders – and have added a pretty empowering tool you can use too!

Let's do a quick recap of *the* most important essentials that absolutely *have* to be in place before we try to implement boundary setting. Until you are actively practising these, or have committed to intentionally working on them, it's pointless trying to cut corners with other 'discipline techniques'.

1. Your relationship with your child should always be your most essential focus. I wish I could skywrite this. The stronger our relationship with our children and the more deeply we are connected to them, the easier it is to guide them and the more likely they are going to cooperate and listen, simply because they trust us. Children are born (neurologically wired) to please and to attach to us. They like disruptions in the relationship even less than we do. This may seem difficult to believe, but the more you use all the ideas in this book, and in doing so ensure the strongest relationship you can have with your children, you're going to find that they require after-the-fact limit setting far less. When you're focused on this relationship, most of the time, your children will look to you to lead them and they will follow your example before they push the boundary for any reason.

2. Remember how important it is to role-model what you want to see in your children. You can't be advocating a household where kindness is the primary value, but be inflexible in your expectations of your children, be judgemental about your work colleagues and hurl insults at the neighbour's barking dog.

I've said this before, but it's so important that I am going to say it ONE more time:

BE WHO YOU WANT YOUR CHILDREN TO BECOME.

3. *Your* emotional space and *your* mental health are key
to you being able to put boundaries in place gently
and compassionately without being triggered by
'your baggage'. Unless we as parents are in a healthy
emotional space, it's impossible to determine whether
our children's boundary-pushing and limit-crossing are
because of our 'head space', their developmental stage or
an emotional need. So once again – prioritise YOU. If we
don't, there are so many reasons we really cannot parent
in the way our children need us to. And we certainly
cannot show up for our children's needs when we
haven't first met our own. (I call it the ETS – Empty
Tank Syndrome.)

4. Rethink your expectations according to your child's age
and developmental stage. Be realistic. Losing your cool
when your toddler throws food at you is not a rational
response from your side and is only reinforcing what
dysregulation looks like. (Part of the joy of toddlerhood
is realising that 'I am an independent little being who
actually *can* throw food after squishing it up and get an
interesting response out of my mom or dad!')

Kids are going to be kids. They are *meant* to be kids. Simply because
they *are* kids. Their brains are still developing (until their mid-20s,
remember!). Too often we punish our children for being exactly who
they are meant to be ... KIDS. We punish them either because our
expectations of them are completely unfair from a developmental
perspective (remember: we are *not* raising mini-adults), or *our*
emotional space is dysregulated and we react because we are
triggered (our stuff, not our children's behaviour).

Really important point: When we punish behaviour that is developmentally normal for children, it leads them to suppress their emotions, to feel like who they are is intolerable to us, and to hold on to beliefs (that become lifelong negative self-talk) of 'I am not worthy' and 'I am not good enough'. I see this too often in the patients I work with. Sadly, when a child is punished for being a child and therefore believes they are 'bad', the result is always the same ... depression.

5. When we discipline, we need to be mindful of not controlling the behaviour NOW. Our attention needs to be on guiding, leading and keeping in mind the adult we want our child to become. (This is where the growth mindset of Attribute 17 comes in.)

This, of course, ALL goes out the window in an emergency life-or-death/serious-injury scenario. When your child is about to run across the road or stick their hand on a fire grid, obviously you're going to be 'that' screaming banshee that yells a loud and immediate 'NO!' before leaping into the situation and forcibly retrieving your child due to your own survival and fear instincts kicking in in that second. In these kind of situations, calmness, gentleness and patience disappear completely – and that's perfectly okay! Use these opportunities-after-the-fact to reflect on your own fears and explain your response to your child. This can actually be a powerful connecting moment between you and your child.

WHAT ABOUT OBEDIENCE?

A question I often like to ask parents is: Are you gaining obedience through fear and control or do your children listen because of the relationship you have with them?

Our children are far more likely to listen to us when they feel heard and respected within a connected relationship.

 CC Moment: Do your children obey you because of threats you make or because they feel respected and heard within the context of a connected relationship?

This seems like a good place to add a little snippet about our expectations of our children's listening abilities and reframing them.

When we ask our kids to do something, we usually expect an immediate response. And we often feel that 'red mist' rising when we don't get that non-verbal 'Sure! I'll snap-right-to-it' reaction.

When you are asking for your child's cooperation, remember the basics:

- ✔ Be in the same room
- ✔ Make eye contact
- ✔ Get their attention first and use their name when asking
- ✔ Ask kindly
- ✔ Keep it simple
- ✔ Be patient! (Their auditory systems are still developing and it can take a little bit longer for the messages to get through and be processed.)

And always, always be realistic. Reframe the scenario: If you were deeply involved in the final episode of your favourite Netflix series and your partner walked into the lounge and asked you to please park your car in the garage, I'm pretty sure you wouldn't smile, immediately leap up, press pause and rush to the driveway to move said car *that very second*! You'd probably say something like, 'Sure, love. As soon as this episode is over.' Or 'I will just now.'

Or you'd agree that you would do it, but would keep watching for another 20 minutes. Whichever way you choose to respond, it's unlikely that your actions would involve immediate compliance, yet isn't that what we too often expect? It's not even that it's not developmentally considerate, it's not 'human considerate'– no matter the age.

 CC Moment: Can you think of any behavioural expectations you have of your children that may not be age-appropriate? (Any times you may have 'mini- adult' expectations?)

GUIDELINES FOR BOUNDARY SETTING

Here are some guideline considerations to keep in mind when it comes to putting down boundaries:

- ✔ As a parent with a fully developed brain, you are the leader, the mentor, the guide. Your children need to feel safe knowing that you are capable of embracing that role, compassionately.
- ✔ You and your child are on the same team. Let go of the 'me versus my child' view. You are standing together, working together, on the same side of the fence, to solve a problem on the other side of the fence. Your child is not the problem.
- ✔ Parent consciously — that means being very aware of which of your child's behaviours trigger you. Breathe and put a pause between your child's behaviour and your response before you react. The reaction without the pause is generally a result of our triggers being pushed unconsciously. (Here's where that 'couch work' for our own journeys and the me-time to reduce our own stress help so much!)

✓ This one is going to require digging deep. Be the bigger person. Our children's behaviours and things they say can trigger our hurt inner child. We all have one of those inner kids inside us. It's easier to draw on our 'rational bigger adult' selves when we are taking care of our mental and physical health. No matter what your child throws your way, as far as possible, respond in love. When your children are triggering hurt in you, it's an indication of how much pain they feel. Take a deep breath, step to one side if you need to. Instead of 'How do I respond to the disrespectful, disobedient, rude (fill in the space with whatever is appropriate) child?' ask yourself, 'What does my child, who is in pain, need for comfort right now?'

✓ Respect your child's autonomy and their unique development. They're not going to think like you, act like you, 'get' your perspective. Understanding someone else's perspective is an 'adult' neurological ability that grows throughout childhood and for some children it's harder to do than others. They are their own person with their own approach and thoughts about life. When we can remember this, it's far easier to approach discipline situations from a 'teamwork' approach.

✓ Don't take the bait. Attribute 15 focuses on this exact point and is particularly important to remember as our children grow into their tween and teen years and become increasingly independent of us. Not everything needs to be responded to or disciplined. If you are raising your children in a home where values are spoken about often, they will be well aware when their behaviour is not aligned with these values. So much more growth happens in a relationship that is preserved when 'bad behavioural situations' can be reflected on in calm states when everyone is regulated again.

WHY IS SPACE SO IMPORTANT IN DISCIPLINE?

Intentional, growth-minded discipline (remember: that means leading and guiding) begins by putting a SPACE between your child's behaviour and your response to it.

- ◀ A space (a deep breath and a reminder that whatever is going down in front of you or being hurled your way is *not* personal) allows you to regulate, consider your triggers, consider your child's developmental and emotional state and the *need* behind the behaviour.
- ◀ Discipline means being MINDFUL of the adult you want your child to become, so it's essential that we take that space that will enable us to respond instead of react.

NATURAL CONSEQUENCES

The boundaries that are most in line with gentle parenting (and the ones that help grow the brain) are natural consequences. Natural consequences are the inevitable results of a child's behaviour that happen naturally with no adult interference. Usually, the consequence is something that's imposed by nature or another person who is involved in the issue.

This would be something like if your child refuses to eat the lunch you have made for them they're going to feel extremely hungry a little later, or if your teen loses their temper, slams their bedroom door in anger and gets their finger caught between the door and the frame, a very swollen and bruised digit is likely to be the natural consequence.

Although we never want our children to get even slightly hurt in the process of learning, sometimes it's going to be inevitable.

Guaranteed, your teen will think twice about slamming their door the next time they feel infuriated. (In this case, when everyone is in a state of greater regulation, and when said finger has been attended to, it's a perfect time to chat about healthier and less harmful ways to manage anger!)

Whenever natural consequences can be used, USE THEM!

Natural consequences can seem foreign to us as parents (most of us have the wiring of the 'adult steps in and controls the situation') and, honestly, parent to parent, it's HARD to watch your child make a bad choice and suffer the results of it. But when natural consequences are used properly, and in the right situations, they create an incredible opportunity for our children to develop cognitively, socially and emotionally.

A few of the 'brain skills' that develop when we use natural consequences include:

- Decision-making skills
- Problem-solving skills
- Critical-thinking skills
- Cause-and-effect correlation
- Learning responsibility and coping skills (where parents aren't 'cotton-wooling').

And the best of all is that the parent-child relationship remains connected and the parent is there to guide, to reflect with (even after the consequence) and takes on a mentorship role. The best learning always takes place within the context of a relationship.

When it comes to natural consequences, it's not just the negative outcomes we need to focus on and talk about within our homes. Natural consequences can have positive consequences too. For example, 'I studied hard for that test and I did well.' Both positive and negative consequences are invaluable teaching opportunities for our children.

Examples of natural consequences and how these may play out in our homes:

REMEMBER: Your role is to guide and teach and young children may need a few supportive reminders of what the consequences could be.

Scenario 1: Toys are left outside.

Parent reminder: 'I see your toys are still in the garden. If they stay outside, Bruno could chew them, or if it rains, they'll be ruined.' Natural possible consequence: Child then chooses to pick up the toys or leave them outside. The natural consequence may be that the dog finds some new chew toys!

Reminder for parents of littler ones when it comes to tidying up: Don't just ask them to tidy or tell them what the result might be if they don't do it. Do it with them. Make it fun. Role-model! This is a great opportunity for teaching, and for bonding through connection. And of course they will be reminded that you're on the *same* team as them! When I want my kids to do something like tidy their rooms, I'll get stuck in and help them. They're so much more likely to do the task willingly when we get involved too. (As we all are!)

Natural possible consequence: They have no data until the following month.

Natural possible consequence: They have to stay in class during break-time the next day to complete it.

Natural possible consequence: They fail a test or don't perform well.

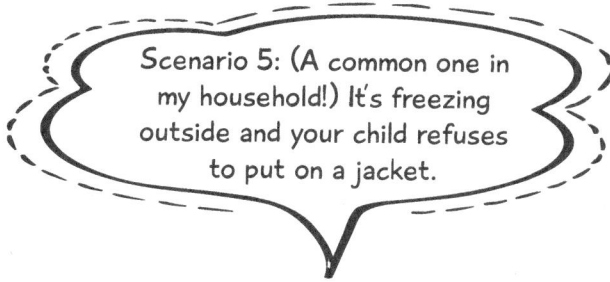

Natural possible consequence: They may feel cold. (I promise you, the next time they won't put up a fight about putting on a jacket! Or perhaps their temperature gauge is completely different to yours.)

Very recently, we were all on our way out for lunch and my daughter didn't want to go back inside and fetch her shoes. While walking in the gardens of the restaurant, she commented, 'Mom, I should have brought my shoes!' I replied, 'Yes, my love, it's always a good idea to bring shoes along just in case. We'll have to remember that for next time.'

No judgement, no 'I told you so!' Just a few moments of reflection and the next time we are heading out and she doesn't want to take shoes, I may just remind her that the last time she decided to go shoeless, she'd wished she'd taken them along.

I could list pages of possible scenarios here, but you get the idea. Notice that the parent-child relationship is not impacted on negatively in any of these scenarios. The parent becomes a mentor. With natural consequences, powerful teaching happens in the reflection time we can have with our children afterwards. As human beings we learn best when we have experienced an event, and its consequences, first hand. Significant brain growth is happening during these times of self-reflection from the youngest age.

Natural consequences, within a parent's guidance, encourage children to tune in, to listen to their physical bodies and their emotional intuition and they empower children to learn to trust themselves. A child who always waits for a parent to tell them what they can and can't do, and never realises that they are capable of making their own decisions, is going to become an insecure adult – not a resilient and independent one. Our children can only trust themselves (a significant component of self-discipline and self-esteem) when they feel that *we* trust them. Easier said than done, but it's an essential part of raising resilient children.

VERY IMPORTANT (RATHER OBVIOUS) REMINDER:

We only use natural consequences when it's safe to do so. You're obviously not going to allow your child to run across the road, your toddler to play with a kitchen knife or your teen to experiment with heroin in order to 'teach them a lesson'. When it's a safety issue, our survival instincts kick in and we yell, scream, jump up and down and do everything a dysregulated parent in distress can imagine to keep their child out of actual harm's way!

FAMILY MEETINGS

When everyone in the family is on the same page about what the values in the household are and what this means relating to limits and expectations from one another, only then can we move on to the next stage in the issue of boundaries.

HOW DO WE COMMUNICATE FAMILY VALUES?

Apart from role-modelling (All.The.Time) it can be a good idea to call a *fun* family meeting. **NOTE:** I added the word 'fun'. You don't want your kids to arrive at a 'meeting' that's going to compare to a boring employee wellness day or fearing that they are about to get grilled with strict regulations. Make it a fun occasion that communicates to them:

1. We are a team working together to make this home as safe and pleasant a place as can be for one another.
2. These are joint decisions. So leave the 'I'm-in-charge-and-you-will-do-as-I-say' mindset. (Actually, that

mindset doesn't belong anywhere in the parenting handbook!)

 Family meetings are great opportunities for each family member to chat about things they would like changed in the family, things they feel the family should work on, and to create perfect spaces for problem-solving and open communication. They also allow for the celebration of accomplishments, talking about things that are working well in the family, discussing things you have appreciated about your children's contribution to the family functioning, deciding on fair distribution of family responsibilities (in my house that's things like feeding cats, setting the dinner table and cleaning bunny cages) and a reminder of individual responsibilities (like letting out the bath water, putting clothes in the laundry basket, making beds and getting school bags ready). Don't underestimate the wisdom that your child is able to offer in these events. I am always amazed by the perceptive comments and suggestions made by my children relating to what they believe will improve our family relationships.

When conducted in the right ways and with the right mindsets, family meetings also enable our children and teens to feel like valued family members who have a voice and are a part of something. Remember the importance of our kids feeling rooted? This is a practical and useful way to help get those roots deep into the ground!

Invite your kids to the meeting in a creative way. One dad I worked with handwrote all his children invitations to a 'tea-and-doughnut' afternoon. Have a create-your-own-pizza evening before or after the chat. Or play a board game as part of the meeting. Let your imagination run riot!

Other ideas to spice things up and loosen the formalities:

- Keep the meetings short and to the point – 15–30 minutes max. (There's nothing quite as boring as a meeting that drags on and on …)

- Don't force kids to be there because that will backfire completely. Instead, try to create an event that everyone *wants* to attend.

- Create a family vision board. Everyone can get stuck in and create a poster that gets put up as a reminder of who you are as a family, what your values are and what you are working towards as a family.

- Choose roles for each family member: note-taker, timekeeper, snack-decider, leader etc.

- Have a 'talking wand' where one person talks at a time and ensures everyone gets a chance to add their opinion.

- Have general rules of respect and courtesy that apply to *everyone.* e.g. No cellphones or other distractions allowed.

- Be kind and keep quiet – those are rules for us parents. You may not agree with what your child is saying, but you need to take deep breaths and ensure that they feel their opinion has been heard.

- Not every issue is going to be resolved before the meeting is over. That's okay. Know that just by creating a family where big issues can be openly talked about without being judged or criticised, you are making a difference in your kids' lives and in your relationship with them. Remember: When our children feel heard, really heard, they are far more likely to listen to our guidance.

REMINDER: Family meetings aren't about giving kids their own way in situations where you know your values will be compromised and when there is the potential for your children to be harmed emotionally or physically. The meetings are about reinforcing that you are working as a team to attempt to solve any issues that may be causing a disconnection, to notice what is working and to build one another up. Family meetings are a wonderful opportunity to share what you appreciate about every other member. It's at family meetings that our family values are reinforced.

CC Moment: What does your everyday life communicate to your children about the values in your home? Do the values you promote in family meetings align with how you are living?

ABC: WHEN YOU NEED MORE THAN NATURAL CONSEQUENCES

But what about when natural consequences aren't an option? Those times that, for whatever reason, it's a non-negotiable for us as parents? These non-negotiable limits are different for all of us. But what we need to remember is that we can set limits while still empowering our children by showing empathy and understanding, stating the boundary clearly and then offering acceptable alternatives.

In my home, a non-negotiable limit involves anything that

my children may really want to engage in that my developed adult brain knows has the potential to harm them physically or psychologically. This is things like watching YouTube channels or Netflix programmes that are age-restricted or where the values don't align with what we teach at home. I'm also a parent who is very particular about where my children have sleepovers.

If you have a young teen, perhaps a non-negotiable would be not allowing them to go to parties where there's no parental supervision (and therefore a much higher likelihood of copious amounts of alcohol and various illegal substances being passed around).

When these situations come up, I use what I call the 'ABC technique'. It's not going to work perfectly every time – no technique is. If your tween is frustrated with a certain boundary you may well be on the receiving end of an eye-roll and there's a good chance that your teen will slam the door in your face, but the ABC approach means there's a far better chance of your child feeling understood and empowered and safe within the boundaries you set. It's a simple acronym that I am hoping you can easily access when you need to.

A – Acknowledge

Acknowledge your children's emotions, in particular anger, sadness and fear, and empathise with them. This is critical for helping them feel understood, loved and connected to when they are feeling dysregulated.

Mirror whatever you feel is going on. Be prepared to miss the mark completely some days. You may just have your child yelling back at you, 'NO! That's not how I feel!' That's okay too. Try to respond along the lines of 'I'm trying hard to understand. Maybe you can tell me what's going on for you right now?' If they're super angry, just hang around until the dust settles and they allow you back 'into their space' to work through whatever is going on.

B – Boundaries

Our children cannot feel loved or secure when we don't have consistent and clearly communicated boundaries in place. These are best decided on by frequently discussing family values together. Remind your kids and teens clearly, simply and unemotionally of the boundaries that have been decided on as a family.

C – Choice

There is empowerment in choice. At the core of all the 'big' emotions (anger, fear, sadness etc.) is DISEMPOWERMENT. When the wheels are falling off, often just by giving choices to our children, within the safety of boundaries, we can help de-escalate just about any situation. (This is definitely one of the most empowering parenting words for me – CHOOSE! And it's just as empowering for our children.)

Using the examples I mentioned, here's what the ABC looks like in action. It can be adapted to kids and teens of all ages.

Example 1: Child is watching an inappropriate programme
A: Acknowledge

'I know you *love* watching this outdoor adventure series.' (By acknowledging it, the message the child gets is 'My mom/dad gets it, they understand'.)

B: Boundary

'The language used in this series doesn't align with our family values and this programme has an age restriction. We only watch shows that we have all agreed are suitable.' (Remind them of the boundary in a clear and unemotional way.)

C: Choice

'You can either watch *Planet Earth*, *Hidden Kingdoms*, or any other programme that is suitable for all ages. Shall we look through the options together or shall I leave you to decide?' (Give them the choice by providing alternatives of what *is* allowed.)

Example 2: Child wants to go to a sleepover
A: Acknowledge
'I know how much you want to have a sleepover with Suzie and that you are very upset that you can't go.' (Acknowledge using a tone of voice that communicates a real understanding of your child's frustration/anger/sadness – whatever fits their emotional state.)

B: Boundary
'Mom and Dad don't know Suzie's parents and until we have had them over and spent more time with the family, you won't be allowed to go for a sleepover.' (Remind them of the boundary.)

C: Choice
'You can invite Suzie for a playdate on Saturday or we can ask her mom if you can have a playdate at her house. You can have a sleepover at Granny's house any time you like. Would you like me to chat to Suzie's mom about a playdate?' (Give them a choice.)

Your child may well feel upset with you. That's okay. When they're in a more regulated space you can chat through the situation and your decisions around it with them. Our kids don't always have to agree and 'high-five' us when we put limits in place. In fact, it's highly unlikely that they will. Our role as parents is to lead, guide and protect. As long as the boundaries we are putting in place are not due to our own insecurities or childhood wounds, and we're implementing them with understanding and empathy, then our children will accept them. Later on they may even thank you! (I mean MUCH later on!)

Example 3: Teen wants to go to a 14-year-old's party

A: Acknowledge

'I know you really want to go to that party and you feel its hugely unfair that all your friends are going and you're not.' (Acknowledge the event and your teen's emotions. It's essential that your tone of voice really communicates understanding and, as you have realised by now, understanding does not mean agreeing with or changing a boundary.)

B: Boundary

'There won't be any supervision at the party and in our family, parental supervision at house parties is a non-negotiable.' (Re-state the boundary established at family meetings where decisions would have been made and explained with everyone in a regulated and calm state.)

C: Choice

'You can invite some friends for a sleepover or I can drop you off for a dinner and a movie at the mall. Or is there something else you'd like to do that will align with the guidelines we discussed at the family meeting?' (Give them a choice. Your teen may not like any of the options, but you're communicating that you are trying to find a fair and safe alternative while taking their emotions into account.)

Then you sit and wait and potentially have some choice language thrown your way. Absorb and absorb *without* reacting. (*#ItsNotPersonal*) Your teen is just reflecting their disappointment in your boundary.

My patient, Peter, who I mentioned at the start of the book wished his mother had said 'No' more often. As a young adult, he knew that his teen self was unable to put these boundaries in place and that he would have been safer and more likely to avoid the pain that led to his addiction if his mom had been able to protect him with 'No'.

THE IMPORTANCE OF THE A

The ABC approach will not be beneficial unless you really get the A part right. The deeper our connection with our children, the easier it is to be in tune with *their* emotional space and to really empathise with it. Practise the A – frequently pause and reflect what your children and teens are feeling. The power of this technique stems from our kids feeling understood, not judged, in their anger, disappointment, sadness and frustrations of life that has not gone exactly as they wanted it to.

For our children to feel understood by us, we need to really work on getting into their worlds and mirror their emotional space with our body language, facial expressions, and tone of voice. When any of us feel understood, we are more opening to listening to other opinions and we naturally become less defensive and more flexible in our thinking. This is exactly what we want when we need to put boundaries in place for our children.

CHANGING BOUNDARIES

Sometimes you're going to become aware that you have put boundaries in place that don't need to be there or limits that you could have been more flexible with. When you've heard your child or teen's side it may be that you recognise that some kind of compromise can be made. Don't be stubborn in these cases. It's okay to acknowledge to your child that you realise you may have been too inflexible and then suggest another way forward.

 CC Moment: Can you think of a time when you knew you had put an unfair boundary in place but didn't want to back down on it?

THE COMPASSIONATE 80–20 RULE

When I talk about the 80–20 parenting rule, I don't want you to think in terms of the textbook statistical meaning of this phenomenon. (Also known as the Pareto principle that *states that roughly 80% of outcomes come from 20% of causes.*)

In terms of parenting, *this* is what I want you to think about regarding the 80–20 rule: It's impossible for *any* of us to get these things right 100% of the time. Absolutely no one can get parenting, boundaries, natural consequences, the ABC and the connection right every minute of every day. It simply isn't humanly possible. Don't aim for 100%.

Overachievers often end up stressed and feeling like failures – battling to bounce back from the times they *do* miss the mark. When you start labelling yourself as a 'not-good-enough' failure of a parent because of those less-than-perfect times, the quality of the connection with your child for the other 80% of the time will be compromised. Leave the guilt at the door. You'll be a far better parent if you can accept that it's okay not to always get it right.

On a 20% day, when you just don't have the capacity for whatever reason to set clear and empathetic limits in place and parent gently, have some compassion with yourself. When you embrace the days you don't get it right, own your humanity and manage to be kind to your human self, you're much more likely to keep persevering on a parenting journey that focuses on connection. If you can't do this you risk abandoning all hope of getting this parenting-boundary thing right. Accepting that 20%, even embracing it as a part of role-modelling the inevitable imperfections of life to your children, is a big plus factor in helping them reframe on the days they mess up.

If you forget EVERYTHING else ...

THE most important message I could ever give you in terms of any boundaries is:

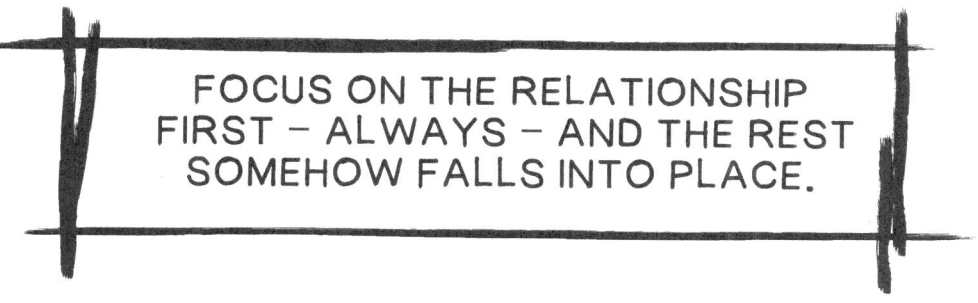

FOCUS ON THE RELATIONSHIP
FIRST – ALWAYS – AND THE REST
SOMEHOW FALLS INTO PLACE.

Top Tips

While I believe that everything written on these pages is *super* important, sometimes it's useful to feel like we are walking away with a few 'powerhouse' key phrases to bank in the forefront of our minds for easy accessibility on those days we just *really* need that extra support.

I encourage you to take a few minutes, reflect on the aspects that you have learnt (or been reminded of) and jot them down here in a CC Moment. There are no right and wrong answers and as we are different human beings with very different children, these 'top tips' are going to be different for all of us.

When I think about the things I draw on most in my daily life, it's probably these – in no particular order (summarising was a *very* hard task for me!):

1. It's not personal. It's really, *really* not.

2. Breathing and sleeping are two very powerful and very necessary components of parenting well.

3. It takes a calm brain to calm an uncalm brain. My state of regulation is essential.

4. My kids are likely just being kids. My state of stress, not their behaviour, determines how I respond to them.

5. When I have no idea how to respond to whatever is going down in front of me, I ask myself, 'What is the kindest thing I can do for my child right now?'

6. The work starts with me and it's an ongoing process. By constantly working to heal myself from my childhood wounds, I am setting my children free.

7. When the big emotions are flowing (as they often do in my home), this is what I always try to communicate through my verbal and non-verbal responses: 'Bring it on – bring me all those overwhelming emotions. They're safe with me and I am here for you.'

8. When I am most pushed away by my children is actually when they most need me to stay nearby. 'Love me when I least deserve it, because that's when I most need it.'

9. Parenting isn't a power struggle. I don't need to control my children or my relationship with them. I don't always need to be 'right'. The parent-child relationship is a messy and beautiful dance. Sometimes we dance in rhythm and other times we stand on one another's toes. But along the way, we connect, have fun and make lifelong memories.

10. I need to always be the person I want my children to become. I cannot expect anything else of them.

11. Saying sorry when I have messed up is one of the most powerful and connecting things I can do in my relationship with my children.

12. When the guilt about being a busy working mom knocks at my door, I remind myself of the power of finding a few moments of uncontaminated connection each day. It's in these times that children feel seen, valued and truly loved.

I asked my kids for their top ten pieces of advice to parents. I was taken aback by their wisdom. Here's what they said – in no particular order:

1. Listen to your children.

2. Don't freak out when they cry.

3. Don't shout at them for no reason.

4. Don't be on your phone all the time when your children are talking to you.

5. Give them as many hugs as possible to cheer them up.

6. Don't ignore your children.

7. Have fun with your children.

8. Always be there for your children when they cry.

9. When they are feeling sad after school, say sorry (in adult terms – empathise) and hug them.

10. Then I asked, 'What should parents do when they feel that their children are misbehaving?' I LOVED their answers:

     My son began: Do NOT give them smacks. Talk to them in a nice way.

     My daughter added: And if they don't want to listen, talk to them again in a nice way.

     That's straight out of the mouths of babes!

These are the takeaways that I find important from what they said:

1. No one likes being shouted at for any reason, at any time.

2. Put all else aside and pay attention.

3. Play and fun are where connection happens.

4. Devices are a danger to connection.

5. Hold the space for big emotions.

6. Hugs and physical nearness give many children a sense of safety.

7. How we speak to our children matters.

8. Listen, empathise, be there. Just be there.

9. Gentle parenting all the way! That's how we raise resilient kids and teens in an upside-down world.

Conclusion

We've covered a lot in this book. Thanks for sticking through it with me. I hope you have had laugh-out-loud moments, cry-out-loud moments and moments where it suddenly all made sense! Here's a few things I want you to remember:

⑩ Ditch the guilt. It doesn't belong with you (and it's super contaminating to any parent-child relationship if you do hang on to it). No matter what has happened in your home before this point, when we know better we do better. (And until we know better we really don't have a clue that we should be doing better or how to do this anyway!) Walk away from the weight of whatever has happened before – all these little one-degree changes and CC moments are the beginning of a whole new journey in your relationship with your child and teen. Personally, I'm excited!

 You are *already* a good-enough parent. Not one single human being on Planet Earth is a perfect parent who has perfect parenting days all through the year. Not one. You're a good-enough parent on a hard journey of life with your good-enough child, and when you see it like that, it kind of takes some pressure off too.

 Along that line, when we embrace our imperfections, we can start having some serious fun. (And remember – there's so much connection happening in fun!) Laugh more than you think you need to. Actually just schedule 15 minutes once a week to laugh as much as you can with your kids. I've tried this and it's AMAZING! Fact: Kids laugh so much more than adults. We need to learn from them. My kids love these 'laugh dates', and so will you. I can promise you, THIS is connecting, this is memorable, and it's really good for everyone's stress levels! (Which of course means more connection and a whole lot more resilience being built! Win-win!)

A few more points before I sign off:
Here's what I have realised from the past decade of parenting and three decades of working with kids and teens. It's something I am reminded of every day:

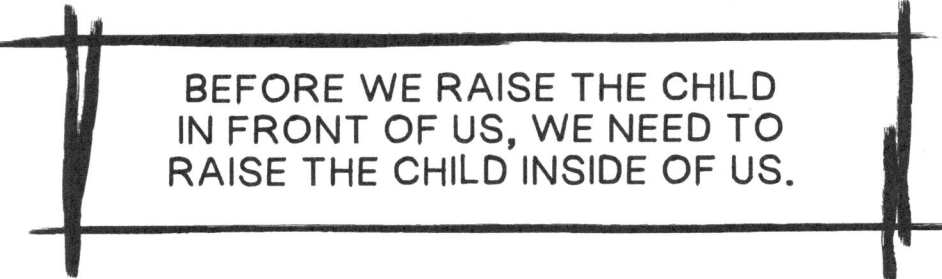

BEFORE WE RAISE THE CHILD
IN FRONT OF US, WE NEED TO
RAISE THE CHILD INSIDE OF US.

It's never our children's responsibility to heal us, but when we open ourselves up to all that we can learn from our children, our own healing is the natural by-product. Parenting has the potential to help us evolve into the best versions of ourselves when we find the bravery to see the world through our children's eyes, to face our failures and allow the journey to make the changes within us. It is only through parenting that we discover all that needs to be healed within us, and in doing that we are afforded the opportunity to become whole and enjoy life at a depth that we would otherwise never have been able to reach.

I challenge you to take a few minutes each evening before your head hits the pillow to consider the lessons your children are teaching you. I can assure you there will be many. Allow these to help you live life to its full, and don't forget to dance along the way.

'OUR CHILDREN CAN BE OUR GREATEST TEACHERS IF WE HUMBLE OURSELVES ENOUGH TO RECEIVE THEIR LESSONS.'

Bryant McGill

The wisdom of children ... Let it teach you. Let it guide you. Let it lead you to being the fullest version of all you can be.

Whenever you get knocked down, in life and in parenting, remember that you have what it takes to get back up. When you parent for connection, your children do too. You've got this! Get bouncing!

With love,
Naomi

References and Resources

Genes for resilience

Niitsu, K., Rice, M. J., et al. (2018). A systematic review of genetic influence on psychological resilience. *Biological Research for Nursing*, 21(1). doi.org/10.1177/1099800418800396

Ground Level

The Economist. (2021, October 11). COVID-19 has led to a sharp increase in depression and anxiety. economist.com/graphic-detail/2021/10/11/covid-19-has-led-to-a-sharp-increase-in-depression-and-anxiety

Kupcova, I., Danisovic, L., Klein, M., & Harsanya, S. (2023, April 11). Effects of the COVID-19 pandemic on mental health, anxiety, and depression. *BMC Psychology*, 11(1). ncbi.nlm.nih.gov/pmc/articles/PMC10088605

World Health Organization. (2022, March 2). COVID-19 pandemic triggers 25% increase in prevalence of anxiety and depression worldwide. who.int/news/item/02-03-2022-covid-19-pandemic-triggers-25-increase-in-prevalence-of-anxiety-and-depression-worldwide

Smith-Garcia, D. (2023, July 21). Understanding the relationship between COVID-19 and depression. *Healthline.* healthline.com/health/depression/depression-after-covid

Resilience, Attachment and Connection
Perry, B. D. (n.d.). *Six Core Strengths for Healthy Child Development: An Overview* [Video]. YouTube. youtube.com/watch?v=skaYWKC6iD4

How to Get the Most Out of This Book
Gallo, C. (2012, July 2). Thomas Jefferson, Steve Jobs, and the rule of 3. *Forbes*. forbes.com/sites/carminegallo/2012/07/02/thomas-jefferson-steve-jobs-and-the-rule-of-3

'But I feel so guilty'
Galinsky, E. (2004–5). Findings from Ask the Children with tips for parents. Families and Work Institute. familiesandwork.org/wp-content/uploads/2025/07/FindingFromATC.pdf

How much sleep is enough?
Centers for Disease Control and Prevention. (2024, May 15). About sleep. cdc.gov/sleep/about/index.html

The importance of normalising emotions
Holdt, N. (2025). EQ cards + EQ toolkit. naomiholdt.com/2025/07/07/eq-cards-eq-toolkit

Getting into the brain
Porges, S. W. (2017). *The pocket guide to the polyvagal theory: The transformative power of feeling safe*. W. W. Norton & Company
   Rosenberg, S. (2017). *Accessing the healing power of the vagus nerve: Self-help exercises for anxiety, depression, trauma, and autism*. Penguin Random House.

Parents of Resilient Children ... Know the Value of Involved Fathers
Chadwick, C. (2011, November 14). Seven minutes a day: The modern-day excuse for a parent. *The National*. thenationalnews.com/lifestyle/comment/seven-minutes-a-day-the-modern-day-excuse-for-a-parent-1.459183

The punishment vs discipline debate
Wikipedia contributors. (n.d.). *Spare the rod*. Wikipedia. wikipedia. org/wiki/Spare_the_rod

Becoming 'bigger'
Hagan, E. (2016, November 19). The "Do You Know" 20 questions about family stories. *Psychology Today*. psychologytoday.com/za/blog/the-stories-our-lives/201611/the-do-you-know-20-questions-about-family-stories

Parents of Resilient Children ... Listen Mindfully
Schicker, A. (n.d.). Consciously here and now. Procrastination.com. procrastination.com/blog/22/consciously-here-and-now-benefits-of-mindfulness

The power of ten minutes
Team ParentCircle (n.d.) Dear parents, just 10 minutes of quality time with your children can mean more than 10 hours. ParentCircle. parentcircle.com/importance-on-how-to-spend-10-minutes-quality-time-with-children/article

'YOU made me shout!'
Marche, S. (2018, September 5). Why you should stop yelling at your kids. *New York Times*. nytimes.com/2018/09/05/well/family/why-you-should-stop-yelling-at-your-kids.html

Further reading
Maté, G. (2019). *When the body says no: The cost of hidden stress*. Vintage Canada.

Maté, G., & Neufeld, G. (2005). *Hold on to your kids: Why parents need to matter more than peers*. Vintage Canada.

Siegel, D., & Bryson, T. P. (2020). *The power of showing up: How parental presence shapes who our kids become and how their brains get wired*. Ballantine Books.

Siegel, D., & Bryson, T. P. (2012). *The whole-brain child: 12 proven strategies to nurture your child's developing mind*. Random House Publishing Group.

Acknowledgements

I am filled with the greatest love and gratitude to so many amazing human beings who have in some way been a part of this writing process. I must admit, rather emotionally, that writing these acknowledgments and reflecting on this journey was one of the hardest parts of writing this entire book, and definitely one of the parts that caused the most tears to well.

To my first teacher – my mom. She taught me to hold on tight, to get back up, to keep on going, to always be kind, to find the light, and to never, ever lose hope. She taught me this through being exactly the person she was – even when all the odds were stacked against her.

To my greatest teachers to date, who arrived decades after my mom left this earth – my two beautiful children, Christian and Rachel. Every day you amaze me. Every day you bless me with the wisdom of your insights. You have taught me how to live life fully. You have loved me more than I could ever have loved myself. I couldn't be a prouder or more grateful mom.

To my big brother and sister, Keith and Doreen. Through all the stormy oceans, you've always had your little sister's back. You believed in me way before I ever believed in myself, and you were the first to say the words I never remember hearing – 'I'm proud of you.' Goodness, I love you both so much, and feel unbelievably grateful to call you my siblings.

To my soul friend, Sharon. It takes a rare human being to be truly over the moon for someone else's successes, and to recognise these in them before they do. For all your love, your belief in me, and

your constant support, thank you. I am blessed to walk this part of life's journey with you.

To Jayde, for *all* the help with edits and, and, and ... (I could go on for pages!), but most importantly, for being my friend, for keeping me laughing (often out loud) along the way, and for cheering for me with all the pom-poms you could muster from the moment you met me. I am forever grateful – for so, so much.

To my patients, young and old, who have taught me so much along the path of life about growth and resilience, and who have allowed me the honour of walking alongside them in their darkness, and then watching them learn to bounce.

To the team at Pan Macmillan South Africa – thank you for first bringing *Bounce* into the world and for your belief in this work from the very beginning.

To Bloomsbury – thank you for giving this book a second life and a wider home. I don't take lightly having this work carried across borders and into new hands, and I am unbelievably grateful for the opportunity to share it with more families around the world.

And a special 'Thank You' to Caroline – for walking this journey with me in such a thoughtful, steady and human way. Your guidance, patience and care through every back-and-forth have meant more than you know. What an exciting privilege to work alongside you to bring this version of *Bounce* to life!

To all of you walking along this not-always-so-easy journey of life and parenting, who have picked up this book and read these words – thank you for choosing to make a difference in your child's life by making a difference in your relationship with them. I can't yell this from high enough rooftops, but I hope you remember it regardless – YOU are changing generations.

With love and gratitude to you all. xx